TOMMY HANRAHAN and RALPH TURNER

IS THERE MERCY FOR ME?

One man's journey from guns and gangs
to a God of grace

malcolm down

PUBLISHING

First published 2023 by Malcolm Down Publishing Ltd.
www.malcolmdown.co.uk

27 26 25 24 23   7 6 5 4 3 2 1

British Library Cataloguing in Publication Data
A catalogue record for this book is available from the British Library.

ISBN 978-1-915046-71-0

Cover design by Esther Kotecha
Art direction by Sarah Grace

Printed in the UK

Some names have been changed to protect identities.
WARNING: Some events recorded in the book relate to child abuse, drugs,
violence, and crime and may be considered unsuitable for some readers.

COMMENDATIONS

Is There Mercy For Me? is a compelling read. It's a fantastic, yet a brutally honest book. Tommy (Hammy) lays it all out there. As I picked it up to read, I found myself unable to put it down. I read it through from start to finish in one go. I found myself wanting to rescue a little boy who went through so much hurt and later wanting to help a man who was a victim of vice and all manner of destructive addictions.

This book has left me in awestruck wonder at the saving, cleansing and atoning power of the precious blood of Christ. Jesus cried 'it is finished' and Tommy was forgiven. Tommy found there was mercy for him at Calvary.

I first met Tommy around twenty years ago when I was a Pastor in Dublin, through his wife Brenda coming to our church to a mission we were holding. We became friends and although we have had Tommy preach and testify at our church, I feel I'm just starting to get to know him in a more personal way after reading *Is There Mercy For Me?*

Tommy and Brenda are a witness to the power of God, to the love of the Lord Jesus Christ and of the grace and mercy which they walk in every day.

I pray this book will be a blessing to many Christians but more so that it will be a witness to those who as yet do not know the Lord Jesus as their own personal saviour.

Is There Mercy For Me? Read it for yourself and see.

Ken Davidson
Senior Pastor, Christ Encounters Tabernacle
Gilford, Northern Ireland

This book is an incredible story of the transforming power of our Lord Jesus Christ, and his amazing grace and mercy in Tommy and Brenda's life.

When Tommy came to us in The Haven, he was a broken man, and life had obviously taken its toll. We will never forget that night when Tommy came to us after watching a DVD, because God had used it to speak to him and convict him that he needed to be saved. That night Tommy knelt and wept his way to Christ in repentance. It's been a privilege to watch the transformation that is taking place in his life and how God is using him and Brenda to minister that same grace to others. I would recommend this book to anyone.

Laurence and Iris Hennessy
The Haven

I have known Tommy for over thirty years and to see the transformation in his life since he encountered the love of Jesus, is nothing short of a miracle! His life's story is a powerful testament to the unfailing love, grace and mercy of God.

This book captures the heart of a loving God whose mercy knows no bounds and whose love reaches into the very depths of our souls. Truly, no one is beyond reach and mercy is available for all.

A very powerful read!

Tracy Buckley
Lead Pastor
D24 Church

Wow, what an amazing life story!

I've known Hammy and Brenda for close to ten years now, and have heard parts of their story, but this book was one of those I could not put down. What an amazing testimony of how Jesus can find us in absolute brokenness and despair and save us so completely. This book is such a powerful, brutal and real expression of God's grace, power and deliverance from the hell and despair that sin creates.

Reading it, I was blown away again by how terrible is sin and its consequences, and by how this worlds only hope is the person of the Lord Jesus.

I've had the privilege of preaching into their amazing church and have seen first-hand how their lives and preaching has found and saved so many others who, like them and myself, needed God's grace, revealed in His Son by the power of the Holy Spirit. I count it such a joy and privilege to be partnering with them in the gospel, through Four12Global, and to be working alongside them as we disciple nations to our Lord.

I pray that this book goes far and wide and that those who read it will experience first-hand – as we did – the love and power of our redeeming God.

Andrew Selley
Leading Elder, Joshua Generation Church (South Africa)
Leading Apostle, Four12 partnership of churches worldwide

In a page-turning, no holds barred biography that you won't be able to put down, my faith has been raised, reminding me that no one and no situation is beyond the reach of our loving Saviour!

Abuse, gangs, drugs, violence, guns, prison was a way of life – but when Jesus breaks through everything is transformed.

'Hammy' today leads a growing and vibrant church in one of the most desperate and heart-breaking housing estates in Dublin, where lives are being transformed to the glory of God.

Is There Mercy For Me? is a must read for everyone.

Jonathan Stanfield
Lead Pastor
Living Hope, Isle of Man

Salvation – that's the word that comes to mind when I read Tommy's story. Not in the religious sense, but practically, how God can walk through the scrap yard of written-off lives and salvage them, renewing and restoring. So much so, that life becomes brand new and unrecognisable. That's the picture you will see as you read these pages.

Tommy's story is evidence that there is a God, a God who salvages a life and uses it to His glory.

Peter Nemhard
Lead Pastor, Arc Church
Forest Gate, London

THANK YOU

Thank you from Tommy ...

First and foremost, I would like to thank my Lord and Saviour Jesus Christ to whom I owe everything. Without Him I am nothing.

Secondly, thank you to my beautiful wife Brenda, I love her dearly. She really is my soulmate. Brenda has put up with so much over the years. Her prayers and intercession have played such a big part in bringing me into freedom. Thanks also to my children who have put up with me – my sons and daughters, thank you all for forgiving me and accepting me as your father.

Thank you to Firebrand Church, Tallaght, my friends and my support.

Thank you to Ralph and Roh for the hours they have spent crafting the story, and thank you to Malcolm and the publishing team. Finally, to everyone who played a part in this book, thank you all.

Thank you from Ralph ...

As is always the case when you write, there are many more involved. First of all, my thanks to Hammy and Brenda for letting me into their lives, for the brutal honesty and the amazing grace. Thank you too, to Firebrand Christian Church. We loved our visit! Such passion in the worship; lives so obviously changed.

My thanks to Roh, my wife. I appreciate, as always, the support. Thank you for joining me on the Dublin adventure. I look forward to many more adventures with you.

Thanks to the proof-reading team of Ali Pereira, Alison Leigh and Nathan Turner. You picked up so many errors — what would I do without you! Thank you to Malcolm and Sarah at MDP for your faith in my writing.

To Jonathan Conrathe and all in the Mission24 family, my love and thanks. It's a privilege to serve with you.

Finally, my thanks and appreciation to my friends at Chroma Church. Your passion for Him is a constant tonic, encouraging me to keep on keeping on.

CONTENTS PAGE

FOREWORD

A number of years ago, while in prayer at our Lincolnshire home, I found myself quite unexpectedly crying out to the Lord for Ireland. I began to ask Him to open a door for me to minister the Good News of Jesus to the people of that land. It was not a prayer that I had planned to pray, but rather a powerful outflow of desire towards God. Little did I know how that prayer would be answered!

I had been invited, amongst others ministers, to speak at a conference convened by Steve Uppal in Wolverhampton. It was a powerful time. I was not aware that Tommy and his wife, Brenda, were attending the event, but after getting home, just two weeks after my prayer encounter in Lincolnshire, I received an email from Ireland, inviting me to come and minister for a weekend in a new church plant led by Tommy and Brenda Hanrahan in Tallaght, Dublin. I had no idea what kind of situation I was stepping into.

As I approached the tiny community hall where we were gathering for the first night of meetings with the fledgling 'Firebrand Church', I looked down at the pavement to see a pool of blood on the ground. Tommy said to me, 'Mind your step, Jon, a man was murdered there last night.' I quickly realised what kind of area I had come to. But that said, when I got inside and was met by fellow believers, saved out of all kinds of backgrounds, I found hearts ablaze with God's love, deeply grateful for what Jesus had done for them, and hungry to hear what the Lord wanted to say to them through His Word that night. The Holy Spirit moved powerfully, prophetic words were spoken, the sick were healed, tears flowed. Over the weekend the miracles increased, many responded to the call of salvation, and the young church was encouraged.

On my second visit, I brought some of my team with me and we taught the church through our 'Impact training course' which helps lay foundations for Christian life and ministry in the lives of believers. There are some powerful truths expressed in the course, notably that all believing followers of Christ can do the same works, the same miracles that Jesus did. Tommy, Brenda, and the precious people of Firebrand Church believed it, stepped out in faith, and started seeing the same miracles, healings, and deliverances that they had witnessed when the team and I had been ministering amongst them. Today, such ministry is a regular feature of the church's gatherings and outreach. They are genuinely 'on fire' for God and the work of His Kingdom.

Before reading this book that Ralph Turner has done such an excellent job of creating, through extensive interviews with Tommy and Brenda, I knew something of Tommy's background, but nowhere near the raw and gritty realities of what you are about to read. This is an honest, at times heart-wrenching read.

I can testify to the very genuine transformation that has taken place in Tommy's life through the amazing grace and power of God. The Prophet Zechariah had a vision of Joshua, the High Priest, standing in the Presence of

God, while satan stood by accusing him (Zechariah 3:1-2). Suddenly he hears the Lord rebuke satan, saying, '... is this not a brand plucked from the fire?' Tommy Hanrahan is truly such a man, plucked from the fire, hence the name 'Firebrand Church'. Anyone who has had the joy, as I have, of ministering amongst ex-addicts and has seen how lavishly and gratefully they worship Jesus can testify of how 'on fire' for Him they are. They know what they've been saved from!

John Newton, the Slave Trader turned Pastor, wrote the now famous hymn 'Amazing Grace', which goes on to say ... 'I once was lost, but now am found, was blind, but now I see.' It's this grace, this 'gift of righteousness' found in Christ, that saves us. It's easy when one reads or hears the testimony of a slave trader, drugs dealer, adulterer, or murderer, to think, 'Well, THEY needed salvation, THEY needed forgiveness ...' failing to remember that the testimony of God is that 'ALL have sinned ...' and therefore we ALL need forgiveness and salvation.

The late Timothy Keller, a well-known Pastor in New York, used the following illustration . . . Two people want to swim across an ocean. One can swim 100 yards, the other 10 miles. But the ocean they want to swim across is 20 miles wide. Each of the swimmers have different abilities, different levels of strength, one appears much better than the other, but neither of them has the capacity to cross the ocean. They will BOTH share the same fate! Failure to appreciate that it took the same gruesome sacrificial death of Jesus to pay the price for the sins of each one of us, whether they be many or few, whether they be grossly immoral or quietly proud, leads to a lukewarm faith, and a perhaps formal commitment to the Christian message. But it's one that lacks the deep gratitude for salvation that leads to passionate worship, fervent prayer, and reckless faith in the cause of the Gospel. In the words of Jesus, 'He who has been forgiven little, loves little, he who has been forgiven much, loves much.' In the light of what it cost Jesus to save us, we have ALL been forgiven MUCH.

As you read this powerful story, may you realise for yourself the greatness of God's love and grace towards every one of us, and indeed towards yourself. May you respond with simple faith in Our Heavenly Father's Love, especially as it is expressed in the redeeming, saving work of Jesus. He died for our sins that we might be forgiven and enjoy eternal life, He became a curse that we might experience the blessings of Abraham, and He was wounded that we might be healed. Paul the Apostle, another great 'trophy of grace', reaches out to us from the pages of the New Testament with this wonderful promise of God, 'if YOU believe in YOUR heart that God raised Jesus from the dead, and if YOU confess with YOUR mouth that "Jesus is Lord", YOU will be saved.' (Romans 10: 9-10). Why don't you take Him up on His promise, put your faith in Jesus, and see what His amazing grace will do in YOUR life? The simple but profound truth is that what God has done for Tommy, He can do for YOU!

Jonathan Conrathe
Founder and Director
Mission24

INTRODUCTION

Things are going well. I've moved away from the gangs and the crime. I'm almost free from my addictions.

As I arrive home that night, there's a smile on my face. It's getting late; the streetlights are on, reflecting against the terraced council house Brenda and I live in.

It's not a bad area. Like any council estate, it has its fair share of problems. But you know who to avoid, you know the places the police are keeping an eye on. Not that I particularly bother about the police. My years in crime have made me immune to them. You get to the point where you don't really care.

I drive my van through the cul-de-sac and onto the lawn outside my house. Best to unload my work tools tonight – it's Halloween and the children around here are a bit more threatening than your average 'trick or treat' kids. They'd just as likely steal the equipment from the van.

I begin to carry in the gear. There's quite a lot of it but with care it will all fit in under the stairs. I can hear Brenda upstairs, putting the three boys to bed. Paul next door is having a bit of a party. Rather loud, but he's a good neighbour.

Another box to bring in. I'm proud of the business I've built up. Roofing. I employ five younger guys nowadays to help me. I've come a long way from those dark days of drugs and crime.

It's as I'm kneeling, fitting in the final box under the stairs, that I see him, silhouetted in the doorway, the streetlight just behind his head. He looks familiar. Wearing a donkey jacket like most of the workmen in Dublin, at first I think it's one of the lads who works for me.

'Are you Tom?' he asks.

I stand up.

'Yes, I'm Tommy,' I say, as I take a step towards him.

I notice he has a rolled-up balaclava on his head. That's a bit odd. And it makes me nervous. Balaclavas are the trademark of the gangsters and the hitmen.

Then I see it. The sawn-off shotgun is pulled out from under the jacket.

I hear the shot. Point blank range. I feel the pain. Straight into my belly.

Looking down, there's not a lot of blood on my T-shirt. Buckshot from one barrel for sure. The other – a homemade dumdum bullet. It's designed to rip your guts out. Not much blood on the outside, a mess on the inside.

The sound of the shot is going around and around in my head. I'm in shock. My legs feel weak. I know what those bullets do. I know I'm dying.

Brenda is screaming now. Neighbours are arriving. Paul from next door is running in through the doorway. There's a phone in his hand. The cops and paramedics are on their way.

There's a screech of tyres as a car drives away.

I stumble over to the lounge chair and lie on it, half on, half off. Gasping for breath now, I grasp my stomach.

Brenda is holding my head in her arms, gently rocking back and forth. I'm going. I'm slipping away.

I feel cold. I feel lonely.

God, give me one more chance.

These last few weeks I've been thinking about God. I've been wondering about my past. This phrase has been running through my head again and again, and it's there again now:

Is there mercy for me? Is there mercy for me . . . ?

I may never know. I'm thinking it's too late now. Too late for mercy. Too late for anything.

By the time the paramedics arrive, I'm in and out of consciousness. As my stretcher slides into the ambulance, I see a tunnel in front of me. I'm dying and I know it.

My life is passing before me, a blur of colour and emotion.

And then, the tunnel.

Chapter One

THE CIDER TREE

Allow me to introduce myself. My name is Thomas Declan Hanrahan. Some people call me Tommy, but you can call me Hammy if you like. It's my nickname from my youth. I guess it should have been 'Hanny' as a shortening of my surname, but my friends decided on Hammy and it stuck. I'm not aware of any relationship to hamsters, but there you go.

Glin Drive is in Northside. As the address suggests, it's in the north of Dublin. We lived in a pretty typical terraced house. Ma and Da, oldest sister Veronica. Then there's Sharon, then me and finally younger brother Tony.

It's traditional in stories like this to start with a happy childhood before you get to the tough stuff. But that's not my story. I hated my childhood. I don't think I had a childhood.

My earliest memories are of Sharon being ill. She had leukaemia and pretty much all of my mother's time centred around Sharon's needs. The rest of us just kept out of the way.

Da wasn't around much. Like many men of his generation, he enjoyed a drink a bit too much and consequently spent his time earning enough at work to spend the evenings at the pub. Maybe this is what made Ma so hard. No hugs or kisses with Ma. If you got too near to her, there was a slap around the head maybe. And not always just her hand. She would pick up whatever was near her and use it as a weapon.

Just like Da, Ma is a product of her time. Her childhood had been difficult, her father died young. And with Da being out of the house so much, life was difficult pretty much from the first days of their marriage.

Ma sent me off to both of my Grans' houses a lot of the time. I loved that. Anything to be away from the head-slaps, the physical and the verbal abuse. Big Gran and Small Gran.

Small Gran was a housekeeper for a solicitor in a posh house. The house was near to the hospital, so Veronica, Tony and I were there a lot, with Ma down the road at the hospital, looking after Sharon.

Big Gran lived in Crumlin, south-west of Dublin city centre. When it came time to return home one time, we didn't have the bus fare, so we walked. As a six-year-old boy, I had to walk the hour-and-a-half journey through the centre of Dublin. Looking back, I'm not sure how I did it. And I'm pretty sure my ma didn't really care. At least, that's how it felt.

On that occasion, I soiled myself. It was such a long walk and there were no toilets along the way. I was beaten black and blue for that one. I found it hard to sleep that night, not being able to lie down in a position that didn't hurt. There was so much anger there with Ma. When she wasn't physically abusing me, it was verbal abuse. I was told all the time that I was no good and would become a worthless person. It hurt me deeply.

Both my Grans drank. Small Gran was an alcoholic, as was her husband. Big Gran, not much better. To be honest, my family tree is a cider tree. Addiction is prominent wherever you look in the family.

Ma was the exception. She never drank. But the anger was worse than the drinking.

Most of my boyhood games were with my other brother and sister. Sharon was so poorly it seemed to me that she was hardly ever at home. Visits to the hospital were a constant in our lives. But that's not to say there wasn't a bond. I loved my sister, and she loved me.

Discovery

I was the one that discovered Sharon's body.

One morning, I went into her room. And there she was. No breath in her body, blood running from her nose. Gone.

Sharon's death changed the atmosphere in the house. Da stayed away. Ma became even more aggressive.

And I always felt it was my fault. As a six-year-old boy, I believed it was me that discovered the body. I remember thinking it was my fault. That it must be my fault. From Sharon's death, for many years afterwards, there was a constant pain in my heart. Sometimes, when she was talked about in the family, I would have to leave the house, go around the corner and cry.

Songs would set me off crying too. 'Claire' by Gilbert O'Sullivan was one in particular. It's about a little girl, and even today it instantly brings back memories of Sharon.

Added to that was the feeling that my mother had wanted it to be me that died. I don't remember her saying that, but that's how I felt. Maybe the physical and verbal abuse was finding its way into my psyche, causing me to think so little of myself and my life.

I couldn't seem to celebrate anything. I hated Christmas, I hated birthdays. Even into my adult years, I found it hard to celebrate Christmas and birthdays. Times when I should be happy, but because of my assumed guilt for my sister's death, I felt I couldn't celebrate, I couldn't laugh and enjoy myself. After all, it was my fault . . . Ma was the same. She'd lock herself away in her bedroom rather than celebrate an occasion. She grieved for her daughter every day of her life.

I became more and more of a 'loner', less and less communicative. I felt alone. I felt rejected. I was told on a regular basis that I was a mistake, that I wasn't wanted. These things went deeply into my soul.

It was later that same year that we moved. The memories of Sharon were too raw at the old house. Still aged six, I was now part of a community on St Michael's estate, near the centre of Dublin. At seven years old, I moved to a new primary school, St Michael's.

If I thought life had been hard, it was about to get harder still.

Sometimes I wonder whether I had a label on my back that said something along the lines of 'please abuse this boy'. My mother's physical and verbal abuse was nothing compared to St Michael's.

The school was run by a group called the Christian Brothers. Today, if you type that name into a search engine, I pretty much guarantee that some of the first words you will read relate to the abuse of children.

New Class

My new class was taught by Mr O'Leary. We all found out pretty quickly what he liked to do. And it wasn't teaching.

Mr O'Leary was a sadist. He took immense pleasure in inflicting physical pain. Not just a rap around the knuckles. Not even a flying chalk duster. This was far more serious. The belt would come off with a smile. Buckle end up. Continuous. And for the smallest of things.

We learned not to answer questions in case we were wrong. We learned not to talk, not to give eye contact. Anything could set him off.

But there was worse to come.

The former headmaster had been stepped down from his position but was still helping at the school. He liked young boys.

We were taken into the school hall, told to undress and lie down on the stage. Sometimes one at a time, sometimes a number of us.

He then proceeded to take down his trousers and shout at us.

'You dirty little sinners! You filthy boys! This is your fault. This is what you deserve.'

And then, to my seven-year-old mind, he did something strange. He poured milk into my mouth.

Except it wasn't milk.

Mitching

I remember the morning. Still aged seven, I felt I had had enough. All I could take of the abuse. I think it must be unusual for boys as young as seven to stay away from school, but that's what I did that day. Mitching. That's our word for it. Going on the hop, staying away from school. My heart was pounding as I walked through the school gates. I waved at a friend, shouted out to another, but kept on walking.

At the back of the premises was another gate out onto the back lane. I kept walking.

I was fearful of Mr O'Leary and puzzled by the former headmaster. It was all too much. So, I took to walking in the front gate and right out of the back gate on a regular basis. I'd spend days away from school, playing by the riverbank, walking, getting up to mischief.

I had friends with me, six or seven of us, all of us abused boys. Phoenix Park was nearby, and there was an old war grave cemetery that became a favourite hangout. Sometimes, we'd go down to the train station and hide in the goods vans for a free ride. Other times, we'd snare pigeons, or play in the derelict buildings. Anything other than school. Anything other than abuse.

It wasn't that I was rebellious towards authority, but more the case that I saw that those in authority abused my trust. To my seven-year-old mind, the best thing to do was to avoid that authority altogether.

There was another effect upon me too. Because of the negative words spoken over me by so many in authority, graphically illustrated by the former headmaster, I felt useless. I felt I had let people down. That I shouldn't even be there. I believed the lies and it caused me to want to run.

But where to run? Home was not a safe place. And it was not only my ma's abuse.

One day, Alice, a friend of my mother, was looking after us. She asked me to go with her up to the bedroom. And there, she sexually abused me.

All of this before I had turned eight years of age.

There were so many emotions. Anger. Fear. And just complete confusion.

God was not the answer either, as far as I was concerned. After Sharon's death, Ma had a nervous breakdown and went religiously crazy. She would go to the church building as many as ten times in a single day. She didn't know how to cope with the death and wasn't finding help anywhere else. Ma's side of the family were steeped in superstition. Talk in the family was of banshees and curses, magic and mediums, spiritualists and tealeaf reading.

In the end, Ma turned away from superstition and towards the church. But the church didn't seem to have any answers either, beyond an increase in ritual and confession. How could they countenance my ma's absence from home to sit in a confessional booth for great stretches of every day? From my childlike observations, there was no possible answer to my own problems in turning to God. God was a God of rules and regulation, of oppression and abuse. A God who took my sister and mother away. A God of the Christian Brothers.

But where should I look? Who could give me purpose? I began to think that the only way out for me was to join a gang. At least there, I would have identity, friends, a purpose.

Chapter Two

STREET FIGHTER

Thankfully, we moved away from the area of that Christian Brothers school in the end, with a family move to Tallaght. Another council house on another estate, this time in the south of Dublin. Another group of friends, another set of streets. And the start of the gangs.

I was attractive to the gangs – I could fight. It was my ma that taught me. She toughened me up. And at times, I wanted to use what I had learned on my mother. I hated her as a child. I dreamed of hurting her. As a seven-year-old, I even tried to cut her throat one time, with a piece of broken glass. I told her it was because I wanted to see the colour of blood.

The fighting, the blood, the anger, were all beginning to affect my future.

Land of the Dead

In a way, it was no surprise. We lived, and still live, in an area renowned for crime. Even today. Shootings are common. One father lost his life the other day, chasing some youths who had stolen his son's bike. They turned around and shot him dead.

There are murders in the Tallaght area on a regular basis. Very few get solved by the police. In Ireland, the police are the Garda. To the police themselves, it just describes who they are. To those of us on the estates, the name is tantamount to a swear word.

As I walk the streets of Tallaght today, I still see the drug dealers on their bikes. I know of the illegal drug dens and brothels. I see witchcraft and superstition everywhere. It's common. I mentioned my own family and their superstitions. My Aunt Mary even got moved around from place to place by poltergeists as a regular thing.

Tallaght has a mountain. Well, that's what we call it. If you live in Switzerland or Nepal, you may have a different view and call it a big hill! The mountain is the source of a lot of the witchcraft. It's on the spiritual lay lines. There are witchcraft emblems written into the pillars of one of the derelict houses, and others marked on the rocks. There used to be a coven there until recently. Altars set up by witches are regularly destroyed by local pastors.

Down in Tallaght itself, suicides are common too. Weekly. Often carried out at the suicide tree. It's an old beech tree in a small park. Bodies are found on many a morning, hanging from the branches. The park and the surrounding area used to belong to the Freemasons. It's cursed land. If you travel to that area at night, you will see many open bonfires with the youth using the light to smoke weed and drink alcohol. I say, 'if you travel to that area at night', but in fact it's hard to travel there. The busses won't go there after 6:00pm. If you are coming home from work and you live in that area, you are in for a long walk. The whole place feels dark. Even on a sunny day, the area near to the tree is colder somehow.

My family is part of all of this. Within my immediate family, stretching out to my second cousins, we have six murderers and six suicides.

Tallaght. The largest suburb of Dublin. The county town for South Dublin. Around 80,000 people live there today. And, like many a city suburb, we have our fair share of crime and drug abuse. The translated name for Tallaght is 'Land of the Dead' or 'Plague Pit'. And it lives up to its name.

But I want you to know it's not going to stay that way. If you have picked up this book, you will know there is another side to this story. There is a God who changes lives and a God who ultimately changed my life. I want you to know that there will be a new translation for Tallaght in the days to come. Instead of 'Land of the Dead', it will be called 'Land of the Living.'

My story is part of that change. But as a child, there was still a long journey ahead.

Glue

At the age of twelve I arrived at St Mark's, on Cookstown Road in Tallaght. This was a standard secondary school, and I should have been happier there, away from the abuse of the Christian Brothers. But there was a shock for me on day one.

'Hello children, my name is Mr O'Leary.'

It turns out that my new form teacher was the brother of the sadistic teacher from St Michael's, the Christian Brothers school. And my new teacher had the same sadistic tendencies.

What are the chances of having two brothers in different schools as my teachers? What are the chances of such sadistic behaviour continuing in a different school in a different area? But as I said, I may as well have had a label on my school uniform saying, 'please abuse this boy'.

And talking about the uniform, I was so self-conscious of having to wear it. I felt I didn't deserve to wear one. After all, to my mind, I was useless, not a scholar. I used to rip up parts of the uniform so that I didn't have to look so smart.

A combination of the physical abuse and the hatred for the uniform led to me walking out of the school gates.

Mitching. Again.

I was back to my old ways. I reckon I only attended around a month's worth of school over the whole year. No one seemed to care. No one came looking for me. My parents knew but didn't challenge me. Some of the kids noticed.

'Hey, Hammy! Where you'd goin?'

It was Paddy Byrne, leaning against the back wall.

'Never you mind!'

'You mitching Hammy? Can I come with you?'

'No Paddy, go to your classes.'

I was leading by example though – he followed me out of those gates and into drugs in later years.

There were a few of us boys playing truant from St Mark's in those early days. Wacker, Bren, Pauley and me . . . Hammy.

The four of us would find disused factories, abandoned houses, anywhere we could hide. Places to keep out of the rain. The old Pink House next to the Jobestown pub was a favourite. Abandoned, and a good size to hide away in one of the rooms.

Places to sniff glue.

Glue was cheap and accessible. It was Bren that introduced me to it. The effect was mind-numbing. On occasion it gave us a temporary sense of euphoria or even hallucinations. All of it, of course, to take us away from the present. No Mr O'Leary. No physical abuse.

But no learning either. I lost my education to two sadistic brothers called O'Leary.

The Job

'If you're not going to bother with school, you may as well work with me.'

There I was, saying goodbye to school for the last time at the age of thirteen and joining Da with his coal delivery service.

They were hard days, getting up as early as 4:00am and not finishing until 6:00 in the evening, sometimes as late as 10:00pm. But they were great days, too. I was earning. And I was not afraid of hard work.

I was with Da, too. A rare thing, with him being at the pub most of the time. In his strange way, he loved me and cared for me. Unlike Ma, he never hit me or verbally abused me. Those days hauling sacks of coal were good days.

The thing is though, the old fella was corrupt. Completely corrupt.

He owned around eight to ten lorries at any one time, which he kept in his own yard. But most of the lorries were illegal. We would queue at the main coal yard early in the morning for supplies and were you to look closely at the vehicles, you would note the same registration plate on a number of them. No insurance of course. And tax discs were not actually tax discs. If you were on the dole, and most of the workers were claiming illegally, you would get butter vouchers in those days. The voucher looked remarkably like the tax disc. So, again, look closely. Each lorry had a butter voucher on the windscreen.

The vehicles themselves were referred to as 'swimmers' by my da and his mates. Each of them stolen from mainland UK and carried over the Irish Sea – hence the swimming analogy. Were there to be a raid from Customs and Excise – and they were fairly common – we would simply abandon the vehicles and run. We'd buy more stolen swimmers straight away to replace them.

Queuing up in the yard was an education in itself. I met a good number of the more hardened Dublin criminals there. With the coal yard being right on the docks, it was an ideal location for smuggled goods coming through from the ships. They were all involved in fraud. There were smuggled electricals, illegal vehicles, backhanded coal purchases. Most were claiming on the scratcher or the labour, our names for the dole, at the same time.

And these were the more acceptable activities. Some had links to the Irish Republican Army (IRA) and other military organisations.

My Uncle Barry was one of them. He was a strong republican and involved in illegal IRA activities. I found myself working with Uncle Barry quite often and was subject to a regular tirade against the British, against the establishment generally, and particularly against the separation of Northern Ireland.

In the end, I had to stop working with Uncle Barry. He was caught with Semtex, working with the IRA, and went to prison because of it.

The Crossroads

There really wasn't much to do in Tallaght. I'd hang around on the streets, getting into trouble. As kids, we'd be shoplifting, aggravating the neighbours and the vigilantes. The vigilantes were groups of men and women trying to keep drug dealers out of the area. They would sit at campfires all night, blocking off the entries to the estate. We would get a particular pleasure out of wrecking their barriers.

If it had stopped at that level of trouble, maybe my life would have been different.

My da saw the need for something in Tallaght to try and keep us boys off the street, so along with some mates, he set up a boxing club at a local community centre. The Sacred Heart Boxing Club.

I was one of the first boys to sign up. I was good too. I could already fight. But this was different. The ring. The gloves. The adrenaline pumping as you went up against boys bigger than you were.

And I loved it. Training four or five times a week, it led to four best boxer awards and a few county championship awards. Out of sixty-eight fights while I was at the club, I only lost nine. And at least four of those were fixed fights.

I was never professional. But it was a possibility.

I made a whole new set of friends at that club as well. Boys who loved sport. Boys who, for the most part, were not in gangs and not involved in crime.

As I reached my fifteenth birthday, I had a choice to make. Go with the boxing friends, or stay with my old school friends Wacker, Bren and Pauley. Embrace a life of sport and clean living. Or steal, sniff glue and fight on the streets.

Me being the genius I thought I was, I chose the streets.

If only I had listened to the counsel of others. If only I had considered for a moment the choice I was making. But I didn't, and at fifteen, I left boxing and started a gang with my old school mates.

In a way, the decision had been made for me the moment I started working with Da. The criminals and gang members I was meeting from the age of thirteen on that coal round were my heroes. All I wanted at that age was to be like them. I aspired to be a gangster. In a way, I was bred to be a gangster.

The boxing nearly took me away from that. But not quite.

'Hammy, we've got a stack of glue! Pauley stole it from the hardware store. See you down the shed in half an hour.'

It was Wacker calling over at the house. I crept out of the door, being careful not to alert anyone.

In the months – the years – that followed, I don't remember that much. A numbness. A sense of not quite being there. I still worked with Da's coal business, and I carried on, seemingly as normal.

But I wasn't normal. Far from it. Glue sniffing. Petrol sniffing. And when we couldn't get glue or petrol, we stole Benylin and Actifed and got high on cough mixture. After a while this led to taking acid – LSD. Hiding out in derelict houses, sheds or alleyways, the hours passed in a kind of haze. So did the days. So did the years.

But the move onto taking acid meant the need for money. The gang life took another turn as the four of us embarked on a life of crime to feed our growing drug habit.

Stealing Cars

At the start it was shoplifting and stealing from parked cars. But the progression to actual car theft was pretty rapid. Sometimes it was just a joy ride. Other times it was stealing to sell on.

And it wasn't long before we were caught.

We were out of our local area, and because of that, not so aware of the places the Garda kept watch.

We'd stolen a car in order to buy alcohol from another area of Dublin where we were not known. Wacker was driving on this particular occasion. Without a licence. Without having taken a test. And still only fifteen years old.

'Wacker! Hammy! Garda! Garda!'

It was Bren raising the alarm from the back seat.

We decided to try and outrun them. Racing through the streets was a high in itself, but in the end, we were cornered. I was eventually caught hiding in someone's coal shed.

And I got put away for that one.

St Patrick's Institution

I'd already had a run-in with the law for theft, but as it had been a first offence, I was let off.

Not this time.

My car stealing escapades led me to the St Patrick's Institution for juveniles. There were over 200 of us in there. The Institution was right next to Mountjoy Prison, just to the north of central Dublin. In some ways, St Patrick's was worse than the prison. All that testosterone. All the lads who wanted to act big, to fight to prove themselves.

I kept a pretty low profile and was put onto the C3 landing. This was a particular set of cells run by one of the warders – a Mr Kennedy. Most of the boys on this landing were from the south of the city as I was, so I knew them. It was a good place to be, if it can be said that being in an institution could be good.

But Mr Kennedy didn't like me. At first, I thought it was just Mr Kennedy's sense of humour. He'd open my cell in the morning with the words. 'Morning Hanrahan, you ugly git. You are just so disgusting!' And then he'd be gone to the next cell.

I smiled at first, but his aggression was real, and it got to me. I'd been rejected all of my life and Mr Kennedy's behaviour fed into the lies I believed about myself. I *was* good for nothing. I *was* ugly. I *would* always be a gangster because there was no other way for me.

In the end, the hatred got so intense, Mr Kennedy put me off his landing and I joined Mr Duffy's landing, D2. This was a landing mainly of town boys from the inner city. I didn't know them well and wanted to be back with my mates on C3. But D2 proved to be good for me. Mr Duffy was ex-army, and he ran a tight ship. The corridor was spotless. Our cells were spotless. We learned to be clean, to be disciplined. It did me no harm.

In the end, I was let back onto C3 and my relationship with Mr Kennedy improved. He began to like me.

The time in St Patrick's was good for me. I exercised and stayed fit. I learned to read and write to a higher standard, to add and to subtract. In fact, my studying was so successful, I got to the point of taking the exams that I had missed through my time away from school. Well, I would have taken the exams, but the teachers decided to go on strike at the moment they were due.

My studies gave me a better view of life and, if I had been more sensible, it could have led to a life away from crime once I was out. But the call of the gangs was strong and within a few days I was back to glue sniffing and car stealing.

The gang itself grew. From the four of us, there were eventually about fifty in our gang. My old schoolfriend Paddy Byrne was with us, and plenty of girls hung around as well. I was one of the main leaders and we kept a close control of the streets we 'owned'.

Gang fights were common and welcomed by most of us. It was a way of letting off steam and usually, no one would get badly hurt. We'd make up excuses to fight, we'd be looking for trouble.

But it was crime that got me into the most trouble. I began to develop a pattern of gangs, drugs and crime, followed by St Patrick's and studies, over the two to three years that followed.

The Early House

'Son, you've got a job to do.'

Da was at my bedroom door.

'Tomorrow morning you're coming with me, Uncle Barry and a couple of others to the early house on the docks. There's a toerag there we need to deal with. You'll have the knife.'

I felt proud that Da was entrusting me with such a task. This would be my first murder. I was to be given a knife and a balaclava, to wait in the early house until this man arrived, and to cut his throat.

Early houses were common near the docks. These were essentially pubs with early opening hours to fit in with the working schedules and arrival times of the sailors and dock workers.

My heart was racing. I sat there at the bar room table with my da, my uncle and two other men. This was it. This was to be a moment I could prove myself. A time to grow up. A time to become a hardened criminal. Just like the men I'd met at the coal yard and on the streets. It was what I'd always wanted to be. What I'd aspired to as a kid. I could be one too. I could be just like them.

I wanted Da's approval. In stepping up to carry out this murder, I had already gained it. I could have said 'no', but this was gangster life. This was what I'd sought after.

The man in question had raped a cousin of mine and the sentence from my da and his friends was the death penalty.

We waited. And waited.

He didn't show.

Maybe someone had warned him. Maybe he was away on a job. Whatever the reason, I was spared murdering a man whilst I was still fifteen. And I'm so grateful.

Girls

Alongside the gangs, there were the girls. I had my first sexual encounter with a girl at age eleven. I believe that the time I was raped by Alice, the friend of my mother, caused something in me to shift. I became sexually aware from such an early age. I wanted girls. I wanted sex.

Eleven years old. I should have been playing with action men and instead, I was playing with girls.

For the most part, it was playing around in the fields, in alleyways, in garden sheds. But as I grew older, things progressed.

Diane was five years older than me. I was fifteen at the time, she was twenty. Matt arrived in this world just before my sixteenth birthday.

It was a watershed moment. At fifteen, I thought my life was over. I had a child. But I was still a child myself. What could I do? How was I supposed to react? How could I care for anyone when glue and drugs were taking care of me?

I went into a bit of a depression. What a crazy world. To be abused, to have my innocence robbed from such an early age. And then it's me bringing a child into the world. Having a child made me feel old before my time. I resented it.

The family on both sides helped and for a while Diane and I got a council house together. It didn't last long though. One crime later and I was back in St Patrick's.

I still called over to see Diane when I was out of prison. And that's when Louise arrived. Two children now. And still a child.

But I was never faithful. I was running around like a mad thing, looking for the next high, whether it be glue sniffing, drugs or girls. In the end, Diane ended it. I don't blame her.

Blame

But I do blame me. At least, at the time I did. I had become a monster. Desperate for another high. Another thrill. Another crime.

It was in my sober moments that I came to my senses occasionally. Surely there must be more to life than this? If I was to blame, who could forgive? Not the God of my mother's Catholic Church, for sure. Not anyone in authority, the way they had treated me. No, I had made my choices, best I live by them.

More fights. More crime. And then I met some of the hardest people in Dublin.

Chapter Three

THE HAND OF PROTECTION

'Did you hurt my son Thomas?'

Ma was out on the street with a gun in her hand. It was a small calibre handgun she kept in the house.

What had tipped her over the edge this time was the state I had returned in. At the time, I had been thrown out of the house and was living down the road with my Aunt Monica. It probably wasn't the wisest of moves by Ma and Da. My aunt let me do whatever I wanted, whenever I wanted. It meant even more fights. One time, I returned to my aunt's house with a knife wound in my back.

On the occasion that caused my ma's reaction, I'd come back to the house having been chased by another gang and beaten up. I was in a poor way, my leg was broken. When Ma saw it, she took action. It may not have been the best thing to do, driving around the streets, pointing a handgun at any lads she found along the way.

It's strange looking back. I would have sworn that Ma had no love for me whatsoever, but there she was seeking out the perpetrators of the crime, defending her boy.

Getting Worse

If it were possible, that time with Aunt Monica was an even worse time for me. I was into LSD by now, craving another high. I'd do anything to get it. Robbery, car theft, illegal work. Anything for enough money for the next high.

And I wasn't afraid to put my weight about to get what I wanted. I was tough. People knew I could fight. The boxing had served me well for the streets. It was rare that I came away in a worse state than the other guy.

I was building a reputation, and it was one I liked. A hard knuckle street fighter. A new generation gangster. Someone that knew how to handle himself and was not to be messed with.

I was proud. Proud of my street fighting abilities, proud of my growing reputation, proud of the gang I was with. And it was this that caused me to step outside of my streets and beyond my ability to win a fight.

It's not his real name – there are still some of his family around so I want to be careful – but let's call him The Boss. He was the hardest man in Dublin.

The Boss

I may have been tough and proud but I was also angry, young and naive. As stupid as most kids are at seventeen. Not a good combination.

It started when my sister Veronica's handbag was stolen. That wouldn't be so bad except that the handbag contained the only photo we had of Sharon, our sister who had died of cancer.

I was going straight. I had cut out the drugs. Alcohol could be a problem, as could my temper, but being away from Dublin was good for me.

Court

The shadow of the Boss was a long one, however. Aileen was called back to Dublin to give evidence on the shooting. I had refused, but Aileen's family prevailed upon her to do so. This was a concern. There could be repercussions.

And then I was set up.

We were back in Dublin for a visit and staying with Aileen's parents. Still getting ready at the start of the day, there was a noise outside.

The Garda burst into the house.

Within moments, they were in the bedroom and handing me a subpoena to appear in court. Somehow, they knew I was in the country and took advantage.

It was dangerous for me to testify against the gunman. On the day of the case, I looked around the courtroom as I took the stand. It was filled with hard men, many of whom I knew were part of the Boss's local mafia. And then I saw him. In the middle of the row sat the Boss himself, wearing his distinctive leather jacket and black T-shirt. Swept back hair and unshaven. He looked like he had the face of an angel. But he was no angel. He was a ruthless criminal. I saw him giving me the hardest of stares. I looked away.

'Yes,' I said, when asked whether the man on the defendant's bench was the one who had opened fire on us.

There was a rumble of displeasure from those seated. A number of the men were now looking at me. Many openly scowling, some mouthing threats and drawing their finger across their neck. I wondered whether I'd make it out alive.

The Garda, having got their man, had no further interest in me and, despite my concerns, offered me no protection. I was on my own.

As I walked through the lobby, looking for Aileen, I saw him. The Boss walked over, a scowl and a frown on his face. He was taller than me. Coming up close, he pressed his body against me, his face inches from mine. I could smell the coffee on his breath.

'You're a dead man, Hanrahan.'

I was foolish enough to reply.

'No, you're the dead man!'

It wasn't a threat I could carry out, and it was so stupid to have said it.

He laughed, took a step back, swung by me, deliberately knocking my shoulder aside as he went. His henchmen followed, a number of them making noose signs as they passed.

We left for Bournemouth again that night.

Breakdown

Bournemouth was a safe haven. The Boss's shadow had reached us, but not his arms. He had long arms, but not that long.

I returned to a semblance of normality, working with Aileen's brothers in the roofing business. The business did well, too. We received a number of contracts up and down the country from the Ministry of Defence to replace and repair roofs in barracks and other government buildings.

I was enjoying the work and, for the first time in a long while, receiving a regular salary. We had a house and a mortgage as a result. I opened a savings account. I became responsible. For a while.

Fiona was born while we were in Bournemouth, and I adored my new daughter. It's fair to say I would do anything for her. I would go to work looking forward to coming home, longing to hold her in my arms, to take her for a walk, to play on the swings, just to be with her.

Normality didn't last that long, though. Raves were taking off in the UK – called 'House Parties' in their early days. I fell in with a group who would travel miles to attend the latest raves held in warehouses and derelict buildings. The music was hypnotic – heavy bass lines and strong drumbeats, techno and house music mixed by DJs who became well known as a result. And raves led to other habits. I became a speed and ecstasy freak. I'd live for the weekend raves, getting high on drugs and alcohol.

Ecstasy distorts your feelings; it heightens them. It makes you feel alive, wild. It also distorts your sense of time – I could spend whole weekends at a rave, and it would seem just a few minutes.

These ecstasy-fuelled absences from home caused Aileen to become withdrawn.

She was unhappy. There was no doubt my raves and drug abuse were taking its toll on our relationship. Things came to a head one night. The arguing was fierce. The results were inevitable.

The very next day, Aileen moved back to Dublin, staying with her sisters.

Fights

I remained in Bournemouth for a further eight months, but there was a financial recession at the time and work was drying up. To help meet the mortgage payments, I invited a couple of local lads to come and live with me. When I say 'local', one was from Italy and one from St Lucia, but both had been in Bournemouth for years.

Toni and Alex were into the rave scene and organised many of them. I joined in, big time. Maybe I was trying to forget Aileen and Fiona. Maybe I was angry. But the outworking of it was not clever.

Constant raves both in people's houses and bigger events in derelict warehouses. Wild dancing, hands raised, heads shaking, for hours on end. The drug taking that went with it. And to pay for it . . . the three of us began to produce counterfeit credit cards and chequebooks. It worked for a while. Our simple premise was that new chequebooks and credit cards were sent through the post. If we could be first to the mailboxes in flats and apartments, we could steal them and use them. We could also copy cheque statement information and pass this on to the black market.

Directly using stolen credit cards could be a problem. You needed to be alert in the shops in case they had a stolen card flagged on their system. On one occasion in the Castlepoint shopping centre, a large complex outside Bournemouth, the sales assistant hesitated as she took the payment. She then began to engage Alex and I in conversation as to where we were from. We realised what was happening and ran just as the police arrived. We later learned that the description the sales assistant gave – one white guy, one black guy – led to the arrest of a couple of other chancers in the same trade.

The drinking and drugs got worse. I wasn't in my right mind a lot of the time. I'd start as early as 6:00am with smoking weed, progressing onto ecstasy and LSD as the day wore on. It is hard to remember much of my time with Toni and Alex. I was in an almost permanent drug-induced haze, interspersed with crime and fighting.

Still with gangster aspirations, I would look for fights. None more so than at a nightclub in Poole.

Poole is just six miles from Bournemouth. It's a squaddie town. At least, that's what I called them. They were Royal Marines – the best of the best. Their local barracks meant that this night club was full of off-duty marines. It was a place we often visited. Despite being thrown out on a number of occasions, they even offered me a job as a bouncer, reflective of my fighting abilities.

On one occasion at the night club, Toni got into an argument with one of squaddies, and it wasn't long before I was joining in. Fuelled by alcohol, I threw the first punch. Others joined in. One lad was particularly keen to take me down.

'Come on then, if you're big enough!' I shouted. 'You squaddies don't have it in you, do you?!'

With that, he lunged at me. As an ex-boxer, it was easy to dodge out of the way, landing a blow to his head as I did so.

He came again. Again, I dodged to the side.

But the third lunge pushed me to the floor. It was then that I did it. I'm not proud of it. I still picture it to this day. It was one of my worst moments.

I bit his ear off. Clean off.

With that, I ran.

The news reports on local radio the next morning were full of it. Police were looking for a man with an Irish accent.

I fled to Dublin the same day.

Chapter Four

POLITICAL HATRED

Back in Dublin, I laid low, fearful that somehow the police in the UK would find me.

I was ashamed of what I'd done. As the fear of capture dissipated and I began to leave the house, it led on to some serious drinking, fed by the shame. And drinking inevitably led to trouble.

Fractured Skull

It wasn't long after I'd arrived back in Dublin that I was invited to a New Year's party. This party was held at a community centre and the idea was that we brought our own alcohol. And to me it looked like most people had.

By the end of the evening, I'd had a lot to drink, but as New Year approached, I felt I should leave. I was back with Aileen at the time. I thought perhaps I should be with her for the New Year. It was as I walked out of the community centre that I noticed my friend Pauley in a fight. Trying to be the helpful friend, I went over and called for the two of them to stop.

'Come on lads, stop it! Stop this stupidity.'

Within a minute, the fight had grown – four or five of us were grappling on the floor. I had one of them in a headlock, but what I didn't notice was somebody coming up behind me. He hit me twice. It was a slash hook, a farm implement. It dug deep into my skull. I looked up in shock. What had just happened?

Blood was pouring down the side of my face. I felt dizzy.

'What was that? What did you just do?'

I tried to get up but fell back. Staring at the ground, the paving stones in front of me, already stained red, were becoming blurry. I passed out.

My skull had been severely damaged. In fact, part of my head had practically fallen in on itself. I was in hospital for three months, in and out of a coma. Two operations led to a required move to another hospital for final treatment, but somehow the administration went astray, and I was left on the ward. The damage had affected my speech so I couldn't alert the staff myself, though I knew something had gone wrong and I had been forgotten.

At best, I could only speak slowly and pretty incoherently, such was the damage to my brain. I felt I was dying and could not alert anyone to my plight. It felt very final. There it was. All that gangster stuff, all the fighting, all the alcohol and drugs and I was reduced to this. An incoherent patient on a ward I was not meant to be on. Unable to communicate, unable to think straight.

It was only when a nurse returned from holiday, recognising I was still there, that the alarm was raised.

'What are you doing here? You could die if you don't have this third operation! We have to get you to the other hospital.'

She saved my life.

I came out eventually, my head still wrapped up in bandages, but decided I must try and get on with the rest of my life.

Aileen and I moved into a squat. It was an abandoned house. I started working as a roofer again, making use of the expertise I had gained in Bournemouth working with Aileen's brothers. I could manage okay, though the amount of bandages on my head meant that I couldn't even wear a hard-hat.

Things still weren't working with Aileen, though. We struggled with our relationship for a while, but in the end I left.

It was the end of our long-term relationship. We did get back together occasionally, and Ellie was the result of one of those times. My fourth child – the second with Aileen.

The Northies

I was sitting at the bar of The Dragon pub when Greg walked in. We knew each other pretty well. He was a known criminal, though he had been sensible enough to keep away from the gangs in our area.

Greg was planning to move to a new area in Dublin and had already met up with some of the hard men from there, keen to work with them.

'Why don't you join me? The stuff you get up to with your gang – it's just so lightweight. This is the real thing. There's a lot of money to be made.'

I agreed to go with him.

We met on their turf, in a bar. It was as I began to talk to them that I realised the kind of men they were. For a start, they had a different accent, and it wasn't hard to identify it as a Belfast one. These were Belfast Catholics, living in Dublin, with a violent political agenda. They were the Northies.

The Northies seemed to me to attract the crazier element that had been thrown out of the IRA – the Irish Republican Army. Not really controlled by anyone, they had opposed the IRA ceasefire in Northern Ireland and had vowed to fight on.

I'm not really that political, and despite the best efforts of my Uncle Barry, I'd never been involved before. But I was involved now. Again, not from a political perspective, but from the point of view of crime. These lads were leading all sorts of illegal initiatives in Dublin and there was good money to be had.

They also had a presence about them. I had been brought up to be a gangster and with the Northies lads, I saw the real thing. A hardness, a determination. A respect. There was no doubt that with this gang, you called the shots. Other criminals deferred to them. Hard men avoided them.

If you wanted to be recognised, to be appreciated in the gang world of Dublin, this was the place to be.

Politics

I may have disliked the politics, but it was hard to avoid. These were not just gangsters, these were politically motivated gangsters. For the most part, each one had a chip on their shoulder. Not just a hatred of the British, but a hatred of the Irish too – they felt that the IRA, and those in the Republic generally, had let them down. At the point when the Troubles were at their height, they felt that the IRA had pulled out, had agreed to a ceasefire at a moment when they should have gone for broke.

These thoughts were foremost in their minds. They seemed to hate everyone. I was there for the profits to be made out of crime. They were there to kill. But I didn't see that at the time, and I was slowly being drawn into their world. Joining with them was a decision I would regret. A decision which nearly cost me my life.

For a while, I was their drug-tester. They were receiving significant amounts of drugs smuggled in from the Netherlands. I was the one to help facilitate the transport and to check the drugs were what they said they were. That meant I was getting drugs for free, which suited me well.

I helped sell arms on the black market as well, sourcing buyers for the guns the Northies were bringing in from Europe and further afield. I became known as one of the more trustworthy members of the unit for my ability to buy and sell.

And I continued to work with credit card fraud. This had become an area of expertise for me, and the gang were happy to make use of that knowledge.

My new life was one of crime and fast living. Daytime crime and night-time highs on speed and ecstasy. All night at the nightclubs.

Occasionally I'd feel I had gone too far with the drugs and alcohol and would retreat to my house in Bournemouth, which I still owned at the time, in order to sober up for a while.

But I always came back. Always to the crime and the drugs. To the bravura of being a known gangster, a fighter to be feared.

My relationship with the Northies lads was never straight forward. I had fights with most of them at one time or another – but with my lifestyle there was nothing particularly strange in that. I was fearful, though, of getting too involved in the dark side of their activities. They were murderers. They carried out honour killings. Politically motivated murders for the cause.

On one occasion, they asked me to accompany them to London to help with a killing. I stood my ground.

'Fellas, I believe in the cause, really I do. But that's as far as it's going to go. I'm not a murderer. Let me help you back here with the drugs and the guns.'

Looking back, I think they were using me. They wanted the target in London to hear a Dublin accent rather than a Belfast one, and if I had gone with them, I think I may have ended up floating in the Thames, a necessary sacrifice for that particular crime.

It was best not to trust them, best to be careful.

I ended up having nothing to do with that side of their operations and did my best not to be around when that kind of talk was taking place. To know too much could be dangerous and I chose to turn away from their clandestine political activities.

Broken Leg

I really wasn't thinking straight. If I had, I would have been away from the Northies, away from their influence, away from their politics. But I stayed around. They helped me feel I was a gangster, a hard man, someone to be feared. I was getting to be a known name in Dublin gangland, and I liked that.

I was part of their gang, but looking back they were really not so supportive of me. On one occasion, I was in a pub with a couple of the Northies lads. At one point I went to the bathroom and, coming back down the stairs, was accused by a woman of pushing her and causing her to fall. It simply wasn't true. She was a troublemaker, but she was shouting loud enough and it wasn't long before the whole pub were aware of what she claimed had happened.

I was in central Dublin at the time, out of my own area, and this was a pub frequented by another gang. They took exception to the fact that I had harmed one of their women. I assured them it simply wasn't true but they weren't about to believe me.

The barman came over.

'Mister, there's going to be trouble if you go out of that door. Some of the lads here are planning to gang up on you. Come round the back. I'll let you out of the back entrance.'

Well, no. I wasn't about to do that either. It seemed to me that there was more chance I'd be killed going out through the back alley then walking out of the front entrance. I asked my friends to go with me. They did, and as we walked out of the pub the trouble began. Somebody started shouting, accusing me of harming their woman. Again, I said I'd done nothing.

A man appeared on my left holding a baseball bat. Another pushed me from the right. I looked around for my friends. They were nowhere to be seen.

Ten . . . fifteen . . . twenty men stood in front of me, pushing me around, kicking me. I fell to the floor under their blows. I could feel the crunch of the bat in my back and then the pain, the sharp pain in my leg as the baseball bat found its mark. My leg was broken. The men were laughing. I got to my feet; crawled, hopped, ran to my car. Getting inside, I was still shouting back. The jeers from the crowd were all I could hear but there was an anger within me. I was going to make them pay. Starting the engine, I turned the car towards the pub, ready to ram it right through the wall. But they'd gone.

Somehow, I drove home that night. My leg got better but there were more scars inside than there were outside. A sense of being let down, a feeling of being abandoned by the men that I chose to work with. Should I really be hanging around with them? Maybe not.

I wondered if I should step away from working with the Northies entirely. They weren't my friends. They had their own agenda. I felt betrayed. I felt alone. If they weren't my people, who were? Was there anyone?

Alone and depressed, I looked at my life. Drugs. Drink. Fights. Crime. Was this who I was? Was this all there was?

I'd like to say I thought about God, that I considered an alternative to the life I had embraced. But to be honest, I didn't. If there was mercy for me, I didn't feel it. I didn't want to know.

I turned back to drink and drugs, finding solace in forgetting for a while all the troubles I had surrounding me.

It was drinking that did for me in the end. Fuelled by alcohol, that was the day I listened. A day that nearly killed me.

The Conversation

Sego was one of the harder Northies lads. He used to pick fights all the time. And I would never say 'no' to a fight! It was pretty 'honours even' in terms of the results and maybe it was the fighting that brought us closer. We'd finish our rivalry with a round of drinks in the pub.

But there was another side to Sego. Greg, who had introduced me to the Northies, warned me but I didn't listen.

'You need to be careful of that man, Hammy, he's left a lot of people up the mountain.'

That was gang language for saying Sego had murdered many people.

'It's okay, Greg. I'm always careful with the conversations. If he starts talking about killing, I walk away.'

There was good reason for that. If Sego thought I knew too much about his killings, it opened me up to be his next victim. There was a truce between us, but no great brotherly love. He was hardened to killing in the same way I was hardened to crime, and that wasn't a good place to be. Killing came too easily for him.

And then it happened. It was after one of our stand-offs. A lot of shouting and swearing, but no actual fight on that occasion. We ended up in a pub just north of the city centre.

Both of us were a bit the worse for wear in terms of taking speed as well as drinking. We'd been chatting happily about the latest theft – a consignment of electrical goods heisted from the back of a lorry.

Sego began to talk about earlier heists and that led on to talking of those he had killed as part of the Northies struggles.

That's when I should have walked away. That's when I had walked away in the past. That's the sensible thing to do.

But the drink was having its effect. Sego was suddenly my best friend in the world, and I let him talk. As he spoke, he mentioned a former acquaintance of mine. I hadn't realised that Sego had been the gunman in that case. I asked him why he had done it.

'He got in the way. He was paranoid, totally paranoid. So paranoid. He just got in the way.' He started to laugh.

I was high on speed. I was struggling with the effects of alcohol. But as I looked at him, I suddenly felt completely sober. There was such a coldness in his eyes. There was no compassion. No thought as to what he'd done. I shivered involuntarily and I wish I'd listened to that inner prompt to run from the place. I should have been out of the pub and away from him at that moment.

I didn't move.

'You know, Hammy, you know sometimes I'm ashamed at what I've done. That kid, that young lad. I can still see his face.'

Remarkably, in front of my eyes, Sego began to cry. I couldn't fathom it. I just couldn't understand. One moment he's laughing that somebody has been killed and in the next breath, he's in tears.

That evening, he admitted he'd killed twenty-six people. Twenty-six had gone up the mountain. And here I was listening to it, high on drugs, affected by alcohol, unable to get out of my seat.

That was a turning point for me. That evening, I began to move away from the Northies. Over time I forgot about them.

But they didn't forget about me.

Chapter Five

BRENDA

I first saw her on a bus. Wacker and I were travelling back home after a night out. She was on her way to work.

Wacker knew her.

I nodded in her direction.

'How you doin'? What's the story?'

I couldn't stop looking at her. So beautiful. A big smile, short dark hair; I was smitten.

You don't believe in love at first sight? Really? It happens.

Brenda didn't live far from us, but we'd never actually met. I knew some of her family. Her dad was in and out of prison. He owned a Ford Escort RS2000. It was magnificent. As kids, my mates and I had considered stealing it on a number of occasions as the keys were often left in the ignition. But no one would dare touch it. He was a known gangster. It really wouldn't have been worth it.

Brenda got off the bus before our stop and, to be honest, I thought that would be the last I saw of her.

'You know, I could never date a woman like that, Wacker. She's just so out of my reach. But, boy, is she beautiful!'

Connection

Then I saw her again. There she was, in the night club. The Safari Nights. One of the worst clubs in Dublin. Sticky floors from the beer spilt. Toilets that you really didn't want to go into.

I was high on speed and ecstasy that night. But not so high as to miss her. She was absolutely beautiful.

She was with her friends in one of the cubicles. I slid in beside her.

'Hello, it's Hammy, isn't it? That's a nice aftershave you're wearing.'

'Thank you. Can I buy you a drink?'

A pretty obvious chat up line to use, looking back. But it worked.

We connected. We really connected. She's my soul mate. She's my wife today. Although back then, I was just grateful for a date!

Our first real date was a couple of days after. Malloy's pub. It was one of the locals. I wasn't exactly pushing the boat out, but it was great to chat. There was less noise than the nightclub, and by the end of the evening, things were getting serious. Brenda really is my soul mate, my helper. She's my everything. I knew it that night. Six weeks later we moved in together. Just a small bedsit in Terenure. Forty minutes away from Tallaght, nearer to the city centre.

Some years later, we eventually married. We travelled up to Edinburgh and married in a registry office. Actually, we had no idea that witnesses were needed as well, so had to rope in a couple of travelling backpackers to help out. No one has ever seen our wedding photos. There's me and Brenda – and two German blokes wearing lederhosen!

Chasing the Dragon

I'd like to say that Brenda changed me. Well, yes, she did change me. But not at first.

I was still working with my da and I was still mixed up with gangs. Worse, I was still on drugs. I was always taking something for my head. In the early days it had been Valium, sleeping tablets, glue or Benylin. I'd moved on to speed and ecstasy. And it was to get worse. Much worse.

I'd been out on a rave weekend. It started on the Friday and by Monday morning, I was a wreck. Delivering coal for Da, I saw my friend Frank along the route. I knew he'd been dabbling in heroin and I'd done everything possible to make sure I didn't go down that track. But coming down from ecstasy can be hard, especially with the new brand that was in town.

Years ago, when I had started taking ecstasy, they were called 'Disco Biscuits'. Pretty lightweight really. But later on, it got replaced by 'White Doves'. White Doves were amazing. What no one realised when these first came to the market was the fact they were laced with heroin. And being laced with heroin, it was harder to come down. You got sick. You got side effects. And that's how I felt that morning.

Frank looked at me quizzically.

'How are you, Hammy?'

'Well to be honest, Frank, I'm a bit of a mess. I'm in bits.'

'Come on in. Take a smoke.'

It was so evident this was heroin. I knew it was heroin. But I didn't stop.

It's called 'chasing the dragon'. Having a smoke to bring you down from the high that you'd been on. But of course, it didn't stop there. Three to four months on and I was using. I was injecting.

If I couldn't get heroin, I'd go onto pharmacy-approved methadone; if I couldn't get that, there was always Napps. These were opiate painkillers for cancer victims, called MST. Produced by Napps Pharmaceuticals, they were easy to get on the streets.

I knew what was happening to me, but I could do nothing about it. Every time I went to the Asylum, the local rave venue, I could see the effect of White Doves. I saw my friend Martin there regularly. We'd laughed together in the past, taking ecstasy. But not now. There was a frown permanently engraved on his face as he slid into heroin addiction.

Martin was typical as to what was happening. There was a different feel about the Asylum compared to the early days. People there were no longer just on a high. There was an edge now. There was an anger. Fights broke out more frequently. The whole ecstasy scene was darker than it had been.

Looking back, I'd say perhaps 95% of the people I knew there moved on to full-blown heroin. That was the effect of White Doves. If ever the devil has a tactic, it was shown at that time. The day I moved on to White Doves. The day I felt sick. The day I chased the dragon.

I was on heroin for the best part of the next ten years. Most of the time, Brenda stayed with me. She didn't have to, but she did. When I was able to, I worked with Da, delivering coal. When things didn't go well there, I moved back into roofing. At one time I set up a small company and had fourteen people working for me. Even on heroin, I was able to work. The company was a genuine one, too. I set up as a sole trader, paid my tax. I so wanted it to be legit.

And I wanted to get away from the drugs. I was completely hooked on heroin. I'd even pawn my tools to get the next fix. When I was paid for work on a Friday, the money was gone by Saturday.

Because of my drug addiction, not every job worked out. But there was enough work in Dublin, so if I burned my bridges in one place, I could always go to another.

Rehab

'Hammy, you need help. You need the kind of help I can't give you. If we've got a future, you have to go to rehab.'

It was a Saturday morning. I'd been on a bender the night before and, as usual, was the worse for wear. Brenda had had enough. She was threatening to leave. The love of my life. I couldn't let that happen; I had to do something. The heroin had got worse and still I did nothing. Eighteen months into our relationship, Thomas arrived. Then Jamie. Then Gavin. At the ages of 23 and 25 respectively, Brenda and I had our three boys.

And I also had a habit.

It was called Cuan Mhuire – Irish for 'Mary's Harbour'. Run by the Sisters of Mercy, this was the only rehab place that would seem willing to take me. Sister Consilio led it, and she was a pretty hard woman. But then I expect she had to be, dealing with the likes of me: 24 years old, a stream of broken relationships in my wake, numerous children, and completely caught up in the drug culture. Something had to give.

I wasn't on my own in that rehab centre. Remarkably, there were some executive types, some senior managers – men who'd made a career in the city. They had money but they were also alcoholics. For the most part, they had been thrown out of the more expensive rehab centres. They'd finished up here, the only place that would take them. At one stage, I ended up in the drying-out room with four top Irish journalists. All four of them alcoholics. There was even a brain surgeon there, able to fix others, but not himself.

The whole place was run by nuns. Under Sister Consilio, we were put to work. We worked hard in the fields, picking potatoes. If we received benefits from the government, they were given to the Sisters. But other than that, there was no charge.

Over the next few years, I ended up in that rehab centre eleven times. One was for a stretch of three months where I worked hard at beating my addictions. But most of the time, I was simply dropped off there. Usually when I'd had an overdose. Overdoses were easy. If I sobered up and came out of the rehab centre, I couldn't help myself. I couldn't resist. Within a day, I was buying drugs. Within two days, I was back on heroin. And every time I took heroin again, there was that overdose. My body had become unused to it. I'd inject, I'd become unconscious, I'd be rescued by one of the family. Dennis, a neighbour of my ma's, would be the one to drive me back down to the rehab centre to start the process all over again.

My final time at Cuan Mhuire was when I broke into the chemist's section. A friend and I cleared the place out. We robbed them of all the methadone they had. Cuan Mhuire was a rehab centre that allowed anybody in. But not me. Not after that.

Laurence

I wasn't alone, though. Not even then. By this time, I'd met Laurence. He was a Christian outreach worker, working for the Stauros Foundation. And he decided he was going to help me.

I'd go over to his place to detox. He'd talk to me. He'd encourage me. He'd allow me to stay. Laurence was a real lifeline.

On one of my stays there, I picked up an old book written by Christian leader Colin Urquhart. It was part biography, about his early life working in community. There was a story of a couple in that community coming off drugs. Colin prayed for them, laid hands on them, and as he did so, asked the Holy Spirit to come and to change them both.

That night the couple slept and awoke completely healed. That's what I wanted. That's what I needed. Was there a God? Would He help me? Could someone pray for me? Could I get out of this vicious cycle I was in, never quite able to break away? Was there mercy for me?

While I was in Cuan Mhuire, I had a Gideons Bible. Not that Sister Consilio approved. When she saw I had it, she threw it to the floor and said that she would have none of that in her place. The reason, I think, was that the Gideons are a Protestant organisation and the Sisters of Mercy are Catholic. For the Sisters, to see it was simply a step too far.

But now, in Laurence's house, I prayed. There's this verse I remembered in the Bible. Something to do with 'taste and see that God is good'. Somehow, as I prayed that evening, I tasted of God. I woke up the next morning feeling completely new. My whole mind and body felt different. It was like a weight had been lifted off me. Looking back, I didn't become a Christian at this time, but God touched me. That night, I tasted Him.

If I thought about it further, in the sober light of day, I still came to the same conclusion. Was there mercy for me? Of course not. How could God ever love somebody who had done all the things that I had done?

Laurence was kind and encouraging. He used to go for walks with me every morning. Generally, I hated the idea of anything at all in the morning! But with a clearer mind, I found that I enjoyed walking with him.

Baptism Before Belief

It was Brenda's mother who became a Christian first. Brenda was quick to follow to church – though not to faith at that time. I promised I'd go along, too, especially after my experience with Laurence. There was something different there. I could see it. I could see it in people's eyes. I didn't yet have a faith, but somehow faith was stirring.

'Living Waters' it was called, a church right in the middle of one of the biggest housing estates in the area. Pastors Chris and Billy were lovely, faithful men of God. They really cared for me. They prayed for me and encouraged me.

Along the way I learned that if you were baptised in water, somehow your old life was buried.

'That's what I need!' I said. 'That's what I need! I must be baptised!'

I had come through a recent detox with Laurence at the time, so was feeling better than average, although I was already back on drugs. The pastors agreed to the baptism.

Laurence didn't. He argued that I wasn't even saved, that I wasn't a Christian. I got mad at him, grabbing him by the neck.

'How dare you say I'm not a Christian! I go to church. I go to the prayer meetings and the Bible studies.'

Of course, that's not what makes you a Christian. But in my pride and arrogance, I wasn't going to have anyone else tell me I couldn't get baptised.

There's a verse in the Bible that says, 'But to all who did receive Him, who believed in His name, He gave the right to become children of God, who were born, not of blood nor of the will of the flesh nor of the will of man, but of God.' This is what makes you a Christian.

I went ahead with the baptism anyway. Baptism before repentance.

The thing is, when I came out of the water, I didn't feel different. And while people were still praising God, thanking Him that I'd been baptised, I crept out of that meeting, found an old friend and injected. While everyone was still worshipping, I went missing.

I knew I couldn't really belong to that fellowship, anyway. They looked different. They acted differently. What was this strange dancing they did in worship? It was just weird. Even their haircuts were old fashioned. It looked like they came from the 1800s.

Meeting God

'Maybe if we move away, honey, maybe if we can just get away from this place, that will help me break the habit.'

We were back home after my baptism. Brenda knew I was stoned. I could never hide it from her. I confessed to taking drugs. Drugs on the day I was baptised! Brenda was in no mood for compromise. She agreed. We rented out our house in Dublin and moved down to County Clare, way down in the west of Ireland. Well away from Dublin. Well away from my friends and acquaintances. Well away from drugs and crime.

It only lasted a few days. It wasn't long before, behind Brenda's back, I was driving the 350 miles to Dublin, to score again.

It was on one of those days when Brenda met Him. I'd left the house early and taken the only money we had, so Brenda was left with three boys, no money, and no food. She was desperate.

In her desperation, Brenda knelt at the side of the bed and prayed.

'God, can you help me? Are you there? Will you help me?'

She asked for a miracle.

As she got up off the floor, she felt led to go to one of her jackets and look in the inside pocket. There she found a €5 note. Enough money to feed the kids. Crying out in thanks to God, it was then that she met Jesus. Or more precisely, He met her.

She realised she'd never really received God's love. Never really been loved at all. Or at least, never accepted any love. She had an amazing family who loved her dearly, but because of her own brokenness, she could simply never receive it.

But at that moment, she felt the whole bedroom filled with the presence of God. Love overwhelmed her. There were moments when she was crying out to God to stop it. It was almost too much. But as the love receded, she'd pray again and say, 'More Lord, more! I need you more!'

From that moment on, darkness left Brenda's life. She stepped into the light. Brenda was instantly changed.

Two days later and I was back home, having not only stocked up on drugs but called in on a couple of raves. As I looked at Brenda, I knew something had happened. I could see it on her. I could see it in her eyes. And I knew. I knew I could no longer use her or manipulate her in the way I had.

Brenda had a strength and power that was obvious, and any 'high' that I could get from drugs could not compare. I could see she had changed. And I knew I needed to. I even started going to church with Brenda. But nothing really changed.

In the end, we moved back to Dublin. It was no use fooling ourselves. Every time I tried to detox, it would only last a day or two and then I'd be quietly driving back to Dublin, ashamed of what I was doing, spending the last of our money on the next score.

As I look back on those days, the predominant feelings were of shame. What was I doing with my life? Why was I doing it? Why couldn't I stop? And I wasn't doing too well with the God stuff either. What Brenda had couldn't be for me. I genuinely thought that God would not want me. Was there mercy for me? Of course not.

Shouting from the Rooftops

For Brenda, it was different. She even had a dream where she saw herself preaching from a mountaintop, shouting from the rooftops, inviting people to know Jesus Christ. How could that happen in practice, though? A brand-new Christian, preaching to others, shouting it from the rooftops?

It was that same day when a couple of politicians called at the house. They asked if there was anything they could do for Brenda.

'Yes,' she said. 'I need a job. Find me a job!'

They invited her to call at their offices and within a week Brenda was working at a local radio station. It was while she was there that she wondered about creating a Christian radio programme. She woke up one morning singing a familiar chorus, declaring that this is the day God had made. And that same day, she went to her manager.

'I would love to do a Christian radio show on this station. What do you think?'

'Why not?'

It turns out that Brenda really was preaching from the rooftops. You see, that radio station was on the roof of the local shopping mall. She was preaching from the rooftop. She was sharing from the mountaintop.

Her radio programme lasted ten years. A young mother, newly saved, already declaring her love for Jesus Christ.

I did my best. I loved the change in Brenda. And I would love to have said that there was a similar change in me. But, of course, it wasn't possible. There was no mercy for me.

I tried. I managed to get off heroin for a while. I avoided my links with the Northies. I tried to work at a straightforward job – and my business did well. I didn't completely get off drugs, but I stabilised with the use of methadone. Maybe things were looking up. Maybe there *was* a change.

Maybe this *was* a new day. Maybe this *could* be the day that the Lord had made.

But then it changed. Nine o'clock in the evening. Halloween night. 1999.

I met a gunman.

Chapter Six

POINT BLANK

It had been a long day. A really long day. I pulled my van up onto the lawn outside the house at about nine o'clock that evening.

I began to unpack my tools. It was Halloween night. Where we live, it was best not to leave anything in the van. Trick or treat with these kids had a more sinister meaning. They would very happily remove everything from the van.

The Bullet

It was as I finished my third trip from the van to the cupboard under the stairs, carefully packing away my tools, that I saw him. Standing in the doorway, he was less than six feet away.

'Are you Tom?'

'Yes, I'm Tommy.'

He was wearing a donkey jacket and a balaclava, but this was rolled up above his head. Looking back, it was clear he knew he was going to kill me, so he wasn't bothered about being identified.

The sawn-off shotgun was swung out from inside his sleeve in a moment. The blast was instant. I fell backwards against the wall, staring with unbelief at what had just happened.

It was so professional; it took just a few seconds. As he ran from the house, I staggered into the lounge, sitting on the side of a chair, shouting for help.

'Brenda, I'm shot! I'm shot!'

I looked down at my T-shirt. There was hardly any blood on it. That told me something. One barrel had been buckshot. The other, something else entirely. This was a dumdum bullet. These carefully crafted bullets are intended to cause maximum harm inside the body, whilst hardly having any effect on the outside.

By now, neighbours were arriving. Three couples from three different houses. They'd heard the noise, even on Halloween night with fireworks going off somewhere nearby. They were aware as to what had happened. Paul from next door has called for the Garda and an ambulance. One of the neighbours noticed that the man stayed in the car he had arrived in. There were two other men with him. It looked as though they were discussing whether to go back into the house and finish the job. I consider my neighbours to be particularly brave. Had the man returned, there would have been more than one dead body on the floor.

One of my neighbours was trying to help with the wound. Brenda was leaning over me, holding my head, praying. Eventually the paramedics arrived. Two teams. They started working on me. I was in and out of consciousness by now.

I knew I was looking into eternity. And I knew it was a lost eternity. I was aware that I was dying. I was certain of it. Moving in and out of consciousness, I sensed I was going in and out of a different realm.

Bible passages were coming back to me, but it felt too late now. I remembered the verse about eternity being put into the hearts of men. But where was God now? Not in my heart. For sure.

The Loneliest Place

In my life I had been depressed on occasions, even suicidal. But facing anxiety and a million and one other problems was nothing compared to that moment in time. I can honestly say, at that instant, I was in the loneliest place I had ever been. I was on the edge of eternity, and I knew it.

Time slowed down. It was just me and God. Me and eternity. It felt like I was slipping away, like I was going into a deep dark tunnel. The only one that could help now was Jesus. I prayed.

'Jesus, if you get me out of this, I will start living right. I will start living for You.'

By the time I was lifted into the ambulance, I had been sedated. Maximum pain killers. In and out of consciousness, I was rushed to hospital.

Over the next three and a half months in hospital, I died on a number of occasions. That's what the staff tell me. I have little recollection of it. I was in an induced coma for a lot of the time. Things got worse when I contracted the

MRSA bug. I remember waking up one night, overwhelmed with fear. It was like death surrounded me. The ward was in darkness. I could feel the hole in my stomach. Worse, I could feel the hole in my life – my life was slipping away.

Looking back, there was a fight for my soul during that time. My body was shutting down. My mind wasn't working properly. I was gripped with fear. I've never experienced anything like it. This was worse than the hardest gang fight, this was more painful than my legs being broken, than my skull being crushed. The fear was so great. It felt so dark.

One night, I woke up to overhear the doctor talking to one of the nurses. 'We can't give him anymore. The sedation isn't working. He's so full of methadone, so full of drugs – it's kicking against all we give him.'

I groaned in fear. I was listening to my own death sentence. And I didn't want to die. I shook in my bed; I couldn't take that news. One of the nurses had to lie next to me, holding me, trying to calm me, trying to stop me from shaking, from groaning. Death was knocking at my door, and I was afraid.

Another time I woke up to find my ma next to me. I was so thirsty. I asked her to go and buy me some 7UP. This was categorically the wrong thing to do. My large bowel had been removed. My smaller bowel was still being operated on. But I was thirsty. So thirsty.

As I drank that can, I was drinking my way back into a coma and nearer to death.

A few days later, the family were called. The duty doctor advised that I was going. Death is a reality for all of us, but for me at that moment, I was facing it – I was facing eternity. Death was upon me.

Miraculously, I lived. In fact, I cheated death four times during that hospital stay.

The Tunnel

That's what the doctors told me: I died four times during the three months I was in hospital. The last time is the most graphic. As my body began to shut down, I felt again like I was going into a tunnel. This time, it felt more like a train tunnel, the kind of tunnel you get on the underground in London. I looked out of the windows and it seemed my life was flashing by me. Everything I'd done, all those hateful moments, that anger, that crime, that foolishness. Everything was flashing by.

I sensed what was coming. I knew this was death and I was about to meet my maker.

As I came out of the tunnel, I saw three people in front of me. They were waving at me, but it wasn't a 'hello' wave. They were warning me. They were telling me to go back. As I gazed ahead, I recognised all three of them. On the left was my cousin, Deborah. Deborah had been paraplegic. She'd never been able to talk or walk and had died at seven years old. But the Deborah I saw that day was able-bodied and full of life.

In the middle was my sister, Sharon. She's the one who had leukaemia and had also died young. But here she was, fully grown. She didn't look sick. In fact, she looked so well, so full of life. And then, next to her was a woman I hardly knew. Her name was Lillian. She had been a missionary and a part of the church I'd started to attend. She had died a few months earlier from cancer, but here she was, looking a lot younger, and not looking in the least bit sick. Lillian had died in her seventies, but as I looked at her, I saw black hair rather than white. She looked no more than thirty or so.

All three of them seemed to be shouting at me, telling me, 'Go back, go back, go back . . .'

I felt myself propelled back to the land of the living. A few moments later, I was coming round in my hospital bed.

'I Want a Bible!'

As I awoke, the first thing I asked for was a Bible. One of the nurses found me a Gideons Bible and I began to read. I still didn't have a Christian faith, but I knew that I so needed Jesus. I sensed He had spared me. I had to learn more. I had to read.

Before I came out of hospital, I had read most of the New Testament. Jesus was fascinating to me. That He had died for the world. That He had died for me.

Or had He? I was still haunted by the thought that I would never be good enough. That His mercy would never reach me.

When I came out of hospital, one of the first things I did was to call on Chris, Lillian's husband. I described what I'd seen. There were tears in Chris's eyes as he told me that's exactly how she had looked when he first met her over forty years earlier.

I then spoke to my aunt and described Deborah to her. Even though Deborah's face was adult in my encounter, she looked so familiar and so like the photograph of a seven-year-old girl that my aunt handed to me.

I'd like to say that experience changed everything. I'd like to say that at that moment I met with Jesus and began to believe. But the fact is that yet again, nothing changed. I still wasn't born again. I had called out to God and He had saved me from death. He had shown mercy, I had seen His goodness.

But still I hesitated.

God had saved me from death. I've seen friends die from a shotgun wound to the leg. I've seen friends die from hitting their head on the floor. I'd seen friends die from stab wounds. But here I was, still here, still breathing. And recovering from a dumdum bullet to the stomach which should have exploded inside me.

God had a plan for me.

There was one wonderful side effect from that time in hospital. I was clean. I was completely off methadone and heroin. In fact, I'd even managed to give up smoking. I'd never felt so good. I kept hold of the Gideon Bible. Psalm 91 was my go-to reference:

'He will deliver you from the snare of the fowler and from the deadly pestilence. He will cover you with His pinions and under His wings you will find refuge.'

For the first time in years, I was a clean man. Out of hospital and able to live a different kind of life. Brenda and I moved house. In fact, Brenda had organised it while I was still in hospital. She didn't want to go back to where the shooting had taken place, so we moved to Baltinglass in County

Wicklow. This is a forty-five-minute drive from Tallaght and miles away from Dublin city. Brenda thought it would be a safe place. A small Irish cottage in the countryside in the middle of nowhere. Unfortunately, it couldn't have been easier for whoever had shot me to find me and finish the job. A cottage well away from prying eyes. No witnesses. Brenda simply didn't realise what she had done. Ironically, the house faced a graveyard.

My body felt new, but my mind was still in fear.

I couldn't sleep. I simply couldn't sleep. There was a fear still holding me – the fear of being found. The fear of a gunman finishing the job. And, in addition, a profound fear of God. A fear of judgement. The thought of Jesus having died for me had faded from my mind. But an intense fear of God and God's judgement remained.

Lack of sleep brought its own additional stresses. I stayed clean, though. Even though the devil has his ways. One day I felt prompted to look behind the wardrobe, and there I found a bottle of methadone. Such a slimy trick from the enemy, but I had the presence of mind to tip the contents down the sink.

Fear continued to grip me. I could only sleep when Brenda was there. Movies describe death as poetic or beautiful. But it's nothing like that. Death is brutal. Death gets into your head and stays there. Death brings a paralysing fear.

I was still reading the Bible. I started to go to church and I found some kind of peace there, but even then, it didn't lead to a clear Christian faith.

Recovery

Recovery was gradual. The wound had nearly killed me. The surgery had been severe. I knew I needed to rest. My body was telling me that. But even so, I went back to work. Too soon.

I had responsibilities. I was running my own company and there were jobs to do. For the most part my team and I were working in Dundalk at that time, at the Xerox factory, sorting a whole collection of new roofing jobs.

I did my best. Really, I did. But I felt so tired. My body was not responding to the hard work as I had hoped. I was working long hours, overseeing the contracts, but by the end of the day, there was little of me left. I'd crawl back to my digs, crash out on the bed and find myself still there, still fully clothed, the next morning.

What to do? How to break out of this downward spiral of tiredness? Something was needed. Anything that would keep me awake, help my body. In the end, I made a decision. It was one that would haunt me for the next three years.

I got into my car and drove back to Tallaght, straight over to one of the heroin dens. What a crazy decision. Just when I had got clean. And here I was, going back into drugs. Back to heroin.

I felt physically sick as I walked into the den. There were people I knew. One of the dealers sat at a table. I saw Martin on the floor in the corner, out for the count. There was Bren, a needle still in his arm, his head pushed back, staring at the ceiling. You'd think these sights would be enough to stop me. They weren't.

'Who Shot Me?'

There was something else I felt I needed to do while I was in Dublin. I needed to try and find out who had shot me and why. I felt it was my best way of staying alive – to try and face up to it.

No one had found out anything, or so they claimed. In our communities, that's really unusual. Gossip is everywhere and it's more than likely you can find out who committed a crime, who broke into a shop, who was fixing drugs. It just wasn't hard. Everyone knew everyone.

But this was different. There'd been no word at all on the streets as to who had shot me.

I had to find out. If there was no news on the streets, nothing from the gangs, no word from rival groups, then it was likely to be something else. Something to do with secret societies and illegal military groups. The Northies. I hadn't had any contact with them for years by now, but I still remembered the times there. The time they tried to get me to murder someone. And especially the time with Sego in the pub, when he had shared with me the number of killings he had carried out.

I swallowed hard and walked back into the Northies house. A two-up, two-down nondescript terrace, you would be forgiven for not noticing it. Of course, that was exactly the idea. On the ground floor, there were some men playing cards. They saw me. One of them dropped their cards on the floor. There was shock on their faces. No one said anything. One of them pointed upstairs.

'He's up there,' he said.

I climbed the stairs slowly, hearing my heavy breathing. Not from climbing the stairs, but for fear of what I was about to do. Up and up. A step at a time.

Two doors faced me on the landing, one shut, one partially open. I pushed on the open door. It was him. Sego.

He was lying on the bed, eyes closed. There he was. The man who had confided so much to me. Countless stories of men and women he'd killed through the years. The one I never should have listened to. The one that I suspected was behind my attempted murder.

As he lifted his head from the pillow, there was complete shock and bewilderment on his face. When you read in a book about somebody's face turning white, I don't know about you, I just don't believe it. I do now.

All colour drained from his face.

'Hey, what's the story?' he said.

I sat on the chair next to the bed, my heart hammering in my chest so loudly that I thought the whole street could hear it. Gripping the arms of the chair for stability, I opened my mouth.

'Tell me, Sego. Tell me. Do you know who shot me? Do you know?'

'Hammy, I haven't heard a thing. Really, I haven't.'

He pushed himself up on the bed, looking away. Looking anywhere but at me.

'But I tell you what, I'll do all I can to find out. Meet me tomorrow night in the alley just at the back here. Let's make it eight o'clock in the evening. I'll see you then. Don't be early. Don't be late. I'll see you at eight o'clock on the button. Hopefully I will have some news for you.'

I knew. Of course, I knew. It was him. It had to be him. Everything in his manner pointed to it. The quietness of the men downstairs, simply staring at me as I left the building. Sego was setting me up. He was planning for eight o'clock tomorrow night to be my last breath.

Two to three years later, I saw that same man on the television. He was being interviewed in a news programme and remarkably he was confessing to many of the things he had done. At one point, he talked of a hitman he used for some of his jobs and a photo came up on the television screen.

There he was. There was the man. My mind returned to the doorway of our house. The rolled-up balaclava. The donkey jacket. The sawn-off shotgun.

It turns out the hitman had been shot himself a year or so back. But if I ever doubted it, now I knew. For sure.

Chapter Seven

ENCOUNTER

My return to heroin was not the end of my story. Things got worse.

Brenda had had enough, and I had to move out. I was in my own flat one night watching a Bruce Willis film, *The Sixth Sense*. It's only right at the end of the movie that you realise the main character played by Bruce Willis was actually dead all along.

The film was a trigger to me in my depressed state. I thought I, too, must be dead. That's really what I thought. With the shootings, the stabbings and all the violence, I had to be dead. I phoned Brenda.

'Brenda, I'm dead. I really am! I'm dead!'

'Don't be silly, Hammy. How can you be dead? You're talking to me.'

'No really. I'm dead. I must be.'

I started to cry.

Brenda came over that night to calm me down. The fact is the drugs were winning, and if I carried on, I would be dead sure enough before too long.

Help came. Doctor Margaret Burke managed the methadone programme in Dublin. On one occasion, when she heard I was in trouble, she actually sent people out looking for me. The case worker found me and brought me into the clinic. They helped me back off drugs. With the careful use of methadone, I slowly came back down. I came back to life. And I came back to Brenda.

It didn't last. Again, it didn't last.

Brenda and I got back together on the Thursday and by Saturday I was celebrating the fact – by taking drugs!

Patterns were repeated. Once again, I found myself homeless. I was empty and I knew I was empty. I needed life. I needed God. But I was still too afraid to take any sort of step in that direction.

Cocaine

Things were about to get even darker.

I went over to what was called a shooting gallery – a house where you could inject. It was run by a lady called Alicia. She sold the drugs. She helped us get a hit, find a vein.

It was as I was leaving the house that I met Dunner the Dealer.

'Hey, what's the story? Hammy, how are you?'

'I'm okay. I could be better. Of course I could. But I'm okay.'

'You look dreadful. Let me help you.'

And with that, he deposited a largish bag of cocaine in my hands. I couldn't believe it. There was a significant High Street value here and he was giving it to me. For free.

But of course, it wasn't really free. Of course, he knew what he was doing. Sure enough, I tried it. Sure enough, I was hooked.

Cocaine is an upper. It brings about a euphoria. Whereas heroin makes you mellow and chills you out, cocaine makes you high. You feel you can do anything. You feel you're invincible.

I felt so good. I felt great. I needed more. More and more. Well beyond anything I could have imagined. I introduced my friend Ian to cocaine, and together we started out on a crime spree. Robbing shops and houses during the day. Breaking into factories at night. Anything to get more money. On one occasion I stole and spent over 40,000 Euros in just two weeks.

Two weeks of cocaine addiction. €40,000 in just two weeks. This was serious.

The problem was I couldn't always find the money, and when that happened there was a real 'downer'. It was like you had died. You so needed a hit. I remember seeing Dunner one time and pleading with him for one little bag of cocaine. The sneer on his face said it all. He was the master now. I was the slave. That bag he'd given me had ruined my life.

I'm simply not judgmental of others when they become drug addicts, especially when it's cocaine. Around our neighbourhood, many of the girls are selling their bodies just to score. I didn't go that far, but I truly understand. I remember a boy I knew. He was three years clear of cocaine. Three years clean. But he could never shake off what he'd done. He had sold his body to feed the habit and the shame of it lay heavy. One night he went home and hung himself.

For me, the habit got worse before it got better. I ended up on the street, unkempt, unshaven, unwashed. Addiction is a curse.

Looking back now, it looks like someone else I see. I didn't care how people looked at me or treated me, so long as they gave me money. I would sleep out on the coldest of nights if it stopped me spending money I could otherwise use on cocaine.

I slept in doorways. My beard grew. My hair was long. I smelt. With just one change of clothes, I smelt a lot.

For three years, I was the slave of cocaine. It took me lower than I knew I could go. It broke my relationships, it abused my friendships, it killed my body.

It's not the end of my story. I'm so glad it isn't. I have more to tell. And a God to be thankful for. Even to this day, my friend, Ian, is sadly still a cocaine addict. He lost a well-paid job. He lost the house, the car. And most of all, he lost his family. Not long ago, he appeared on my doorstep carrying part of a three-piece suite. It had been a gift to his wife for Christmas from her family, but while she was away, he was trying to sell it. Anything to feed the habit.

Cocaine is the devil's weapon. I see it destroying my city today. It nearly destroyed me . . .

Ending it all

'I'm going to end it, Jimmy. I'm going to end it.'

It was New Year's Eve 2001. I was parked up in Aberlay Court Hotel car park. It was one especially used by dropouts and druggies. I was homeless, living in the back of my van.

That evening, Jimmy was with me. He was one of my drug pushers and we were both shooting up cocaine. Of course we were.

On New Year's Eve, it should have been a good time, but here I was crying uncontrollably, thinking about my kids and Brenda back home. Thinking about all the things I'd done. The people I had harmed.

'Jimmy, I hate myself, I hate myself! I hate my life. I hate all this stuff. I hate what it's doing to me. Jimmy, I'm gonna kill myself.'

'Will you give it over, Hammy, you're wrecking my head. Shut up. Just shut up! Stop it! I don't want to hear.'

I cried myself to sleep that night, sitting upright in the front of my van. There was a deep, deep grief within me. It felt like it really was the end. I couldn't go on like this.

In one pocket I had 2,000 Euros. Stolen, of course. In the other pocket, I had enough cocaine for a full night's pleasure. But it's the tears I remember that night. Just the crying, the constant crying.

If you have ever been in that place, you will understand what I am talking about. You get to the point where the drugs just don't work anymore.

In my house, when I'd had a house, I actually had a rope up in the loft, tied already into a noose, ready to be used when I plucked up the courage. That's how low I'd come. That's how deep the despair was.

It was time.

The Devil's Food

By this stage, New Year's Eve 2001, I'd been back on drugs for three years and injecting cocaine for about ten months. I was spending €2,000 a day on the habit and doing anything for it, robbing shops in the daytime, factories at night. I honestly would have sold my wife and kids for that habit. As it was, I stole from my children. I stole from my friends. And I had lost everything.

Everyone had given up on me by now. I was sofa-surfing and living in the van, staying over at crack houses where everyone was smoking crack cocaine and sleeping over. I'd stay at the shooting galleries where everyone was injecting. I'd live on the streets.

Cocaine demoralises you. It's totally demonic. The Greek root for the word witchcraft or sorcery is *pharmakia*. It's the mixing of chemicals for drug induced spells. That's what drugs are. That's what cocaine is. I was deep into death and destruction, witchcraft and sorcery, hooked on the devil's agenda, taking the devil's food.

By the very next day I'd used up all my drug money, I'd finished injecting everything I had on me and had decided not to kill myself just yet. I decided to rip off the local pastor instead. He was a nice guy.

'Pastor Declan, my granny has died. I desperately need money for clothes to go to the funeral. Can you help me?'

'Thomas, would you not get help now?'

'I'm planning on it, Pastor, I'm planning on it, honestly.'

'Why don't you call Laurence? Book yourself into The Haven? You've stayed there before, right? See if he will take you in.'

'Yeah, yeah, I will ... Tomorrow. I'll do it tomorrow.'

'How about now? What if I can call him now?'

'Sure, call him. Yeah, go ahead. So long as I can have that cash for the suit, you know – the suit for the funeral.'

The call was made, and as Pastor Declan passed me the phone, I put on a good show. I said to Laurence that I'd be there tomorrow. I had no intention of doing so, of course. It was all to get the money.

The pastor's money went on more drugs and I went home to Brenda that same evening.

'Brenda, Granny is dying, and I need some more money. I need help to get a suit. And please, will you let me stay home? I need to get my head straight.'

She let me stay, not that she was convinced by the Granny story, of course.

The next day, I really did go over to see Laurence. In my mind, I was thinking maybe I'll stay four days. That's the methadone point. I'll wait until 'cold turkey' starts, I reasoned, and then I'll need to leave, to hit some cocaine. Generally, cocaine is not so hard to come off. But methadone is terrible, and I'd not only been taking cocaine, but I'd continued my use of methadone on prescription. After four days of coming off methadone, you're in a mess. You feel desperately sick, you shake. Your body is screaming for more. I knew that should happen and that was when I would leave The Haven. That was when I'd go back onto the streets. Or worse.

The funny thing is the next day didn't feel too bad. Nor the day after, or the day after that. By the fourth day, I was fully expecting to feel terrible, but I woke up refreshed and alive. It was as if I'd never taken heroin, cocaine or methadone.

That methadone is an unforgiving master. It never lets you get away with taking it. But this time was different. This was the day I had planned to leave – the fourth day. I had a plan. The word of God says that a man makes plans, but the Lord determines his steps. This is so true.

I didn't get sick. I didn't feel sick. Surely cold turkey would kick in soon. Surely the sickness would come. But it didn't.

The Video

I remember Laurence asking me and a couple of others who were staying there to sit and watch a video. It was the story of a man from the Ulster Volunteer Force (UVF). The UVF were the ones I hated most of all – paramilitaries, but on what I'd joke was the dark side, the Protestant side. The man's name was Graham. On the video, he was talking about Jesus. I knew Jesus. Well, I knew all about him anyway. What would be the harm in watching . . . The video continued. 'I picked up on drugs to be a man, but it never made me a man. I picked up on alcohol to make me a man, but it never made me a man. I'd run around with guns to make me a man, but it never made me a man. It was only when I picked up the Bible that I found out I could truly be the man God wanted me to be.'

By now, the other two residents had left the room. Laurence was still there. It was at that point that something hit home. The words continued in my head long after the video had moved on . . . I picked up on drugs to be a man, but it never made me a man. I picked up on alcohol to make me a man, but it never made me a man. I'd run around with guns to make me a man, but it never made me a man . . . That was me. Something was happening on the inside. As I stared at the screen, I fell to my knees.

I'd always prayed. Even in my disbelieving state, I'd always been asking Jesus for something – money, family, jobs. I'd said the 'sinner's prayer' a hundred times by now, but this time was different. Everything stopped. The world seemed to come to a halt.

I found myself crying. Crying uncontrollably. Something was happening inside me. Laurence began to walk out of the room. With my knees shaking, with my whole body in convulsions, I half walked, half crawled out of the lounge and into the hallway.

'Laurence, Laurence! I need forgiveness! I need it. I need to be forgiven. I know what I've been doing is wrong. Oh, Jesus! Jesus, forgive me!'

I fell to the floor.

As I looked up, past Laurence's shoulder, I saw Jesus. On a cross. He was looking at me. Staring at me, looking directly into my heart. In my mind, I should have been feeling judged at that point – condemned, alone, guilty. But all I saw was love. I saw it in His eyes that night. I'd never seen a face like it before. To this day, I see Him and it brings me to tears. That look of complete love. That forgiveness so freely offered.

Lying down in the hallway, I was still screaming; screaming at the top of my voice.

'Jesus, forgive me. Forgive me!'

And it was then, I knew. I knew it was my sin that put Jesus on the cross. Every evil act. Everything I'd done and thought. Every lie. Every factory robbed, every moment of shoplifting, thieving, car stealing, aggression and brutality. Every snort of coke, every injection. It was me that put Jesus on the cross.

Still crying, I pulled myself up from the floor, a brand-new person. My testimony is this – from that moment, I was free. No drug addiction. No cold turkey. No mental health problems. Instant healing from hepatitis caused by the needles. No after-effects at all.

I was free.

Changes

My life changed instantly in that hallway. By now, the other two guests were staring at me, wondering what had happened. The girl there was caught up in drugs and the man was an alcoholic. They didn't understand. But I knew. I knew! I knew from that moment that I would never be the same again. I knew from that moment that life had changed, and changed forever.

That night, as I went to bed, my mind was filled – not with hallucinations, not with drugs, but with Jesus. I sensed the power of the Holy Spirit on me. Looking back, I know now that this was the moment I was baptised in the Holy Spirit. This was the moment that God came upon me in such a mighty way.

I was so filled with Jesus, there was no way I could sleep. I sat up, reading the Bible all night. I grabbed a notebook and pen and began to write the things I heard God saying to me. Things I should do. Things I should change.

Changes were pretty instant. I was eating God's word. That's the only way to put it. I was eating the Bible. Breakfast, dinner and tea. Every moment. Every second I could find I was reading.

And I stopped swearing. That, too, was pretty instant.

I stayed in The Haven for seven weeks. It was a six-week course and I gave myself an extra week. Laurence walked the journey with me, step by step. Most days I would sit at a table, a mug of tea in one hand, a cigarette in the other, and the Bible in front of me.

I would read the words from the Bible. Apply them to my life. Pray out loud. Declare Jesus' victory.

'Hey Hammy, how about we do something?'

It was Laurence putting his head around the door.

'Why don't you write out on a piece of paper everything you can remember. All you've ever said or done that was wrong. Every sin. Capture it all. Ask God to bring it to mind, and then what we'll do, we'll go outside and burn the pages.'

I thought it was a great idea and took three or four pieces of paper from the table. Going into my room, I sat down and began to write. A few minutes later, I was back downstairs, grabbing hold of some extra paper. Thirty pages later and I still hadn't finished. God just kept reminding me of things. Things I'd done. Lies. Stealing. Violence. The drugs. Living on the streets. Everything was there. Everything. All on those pieces of paper.

We took the whole sheaf of them outside. And lit a match.

Scripture Speaking

I'd never completed anything in my life. But I finished the complete detox course at The Haven, with extra time after it as well. There were challenges along the way. The man there kept challenging me – was I really off drugs? Could I really change? I prayed. I stayed on course.

My weekly sessions with Laurence became shorter and shorter. In a sense, I didn't need the counsel as to how to stay off drugs. I was free. Genuinely free. I found myself desperate to finish my counselling sessions in order to get back to the Bible. The Holy Spirit was my teacher. I felt I was in God's personal classroom.

Scripture spoke to me; kept speaking to me. John 14: He that believes will do greater things . . . I could actually do things for God! This itself was a revelation. Psalm 91: He will deliver you from the snare of the fowler and from the deadly pestilence. Psalm 40: I waited patiently for the Lord, he drew me out of the pit. That was me. That was me! I'd been in a pit most of my life. But God pulled me out.

I went home on a high. But it was a very different kind of high. For most of the next year, I sat at home reading the word and worshipping God. I'm not sure Brenda approved entirely. She said I was too heavenly minded to be any earthly use. And there's some truth in that.

We had no money, or at least, little to live off. Occasionally envelopes came through the door from folks at church. I'd be offered a few small jobs and I took them. But mostly, I just wanted to read. Read and read and read again. Every word of scripture was finding a place in my heart.

When Christmas came, we had no money for the kids, but it was just then, after we prayed, that a job came through. It paid for all the Christmas presents that year.

I was excited. For all God had done in me, for the future, for the family. For the first time in living memory, I was free. Free from crime. Free from drink. Free from drugs. Free.

But with freedom comes responsibility. And with such a radical life change there was a lot I needed to learn.

Chapter Eight

LEARNING TO LIVE

One of the oddities of being clean is having to deal with the past. As I left Laurence and returned home, I found the home stay was rather shorter than expected.

Prison

Being clean and being honest meant I was no longer stealing. But I had a debt. A 40,000 Euros debt. In particular, someone was pushing for me to pay €1,500. I couldn't pay it and served a short prison sentence instead. The prison officers thought I might be at risk from other prisoners due to my past and to my newfound honesty. I ended up in a prison cell with a few other security prisoners. One afternoon in the yard, I was called back by one of the officers and told to go to my cell. I arrived to find a young man there, on his own.

As I was shown into the cell, the prison guard made it clear who the lad was. He was a drink driver who had knocked down a kid. There was an expectation by many prison guards that the best way to deal with that particular type of person was for other prisoners to beat them up. If they survive, they learn. If they don't, they deserve it – or so says the law of the prison yard.

I realised that I had been picked out as a known fighter with the bullet wounds to prove it, and I was being introduced to my 'prey'. The guard seemed not to know of my change of life.

As I walked over to the lad, he moved away into the corner of the room, fully expecting to be worked over. Instead, I spoke to him.

'No matter what you have done, son, if you truly repent, Jesus will forgive you.'

It's all I said. The other prisoners returned soon after and the young man was moved to another cell. I don't know how his story ended, but I do know that on a day when he expected rough justice, he was offered God's grace. That alone would be enough reason for me to have served that short extra spell in prison.

Learning

Brenda and I were learning to pray together. But there was tension, too. Up until that point, she'd effectively been head of the home. I'd been no help. How could I have been? I had destroyed my whole life in front of her with my drug use. I didn't know how to be a husband. I didn't know how to be a father. Brenda had done everything.

But then suddenly I'm home and I'm wanting to act the man of the house. I expected to take that role. It wasn't that simple, though. Brenda, quite rightly, had put walls up around her. She had protected herself from me and my excesses, and it would take a while for those walls to come down.

Our past hadn't been exactly encouraging to Brenda. We had both fought physically with each other. One time way back, Brenda attacked me with a hot iron. I had a bare iron-shaped mark on my not-so-hairy chest for some time after! Another time in a hotel, we had made so much noise with our fighting, the manager knocked on our hotel door. I answered it, my nose pouring with blood.

'Is everything alright, sir? I thought I should just check.'

'Yes,' I said. 'No problems, thanks.'

I was impressed that he kept his face entirely passive during the conversation!

A Three Stranded Cord

We prayed more. We talked more. On occasions, we shouted. And once or twice the marriage nearly ended, just with the strain of all that was changing.

But the Bible says a three stranded cord can't be broken. Jesus bound us together. Today, we have an amazing relationship. It feels like I'm on a permanent honeymoon. When I drive down the street and I know I'm going home, I am so looking forward to seeing my wife. There's this wide grin on my face as I park the car in front of the house. I love Brenda as much as on that first day I met her. Even more.

The children have been the hard part. Young Tommy watching me inject. Finding me in the morning with a needle still in my arm. It's affected him. Of course it has.

Not particularly having had a loving father myself, I had to learn how to love as a father. I had to learn to love my children. All of them. The three from my marriage with Brenda. The four from previous relationships. They are all on a journey, but I trust that God has got their hand.

Lack of Wisdom

I felt I was overflowing with the Holy Spirit, but passion doesn't always mean wisdom. I had some understanding of what God had done in my life, but how to work that out within the local church was another matter. My observation of the church was that they were lazy. They didn't seem to want to worship.

I'm so grateful today for pastors Billy and Chris at Living Waters Church, Tallaght. Along with other leaders, such as Laurence and my good friend Sam Lynch, they encouraged me, they put up with me! Without them and without their patience, I'm not sure where I would be. When I had first gone along to church, I just thought them strange. They talked funny, they looked old-fashioned. But they put the word of God into me, and in the ten or so years Brenda and I were at Living Waters, we grew in our faith. And in my darker days, those pastors and leaders wouldn't think twice about chasing me around the drug dens, trying to find me and help me. That's the truth. So when I comment that I thought the worship was lazy – it may have been, but what right did I have to judge? I did though.

Overflowing with a combination of the Holy Spirit and a complete lack of wisdom as to how to respond, I became a bit of a firebrand. A fire had been lit within me and its outworking was on the streets of Tallaght. Outreaches. Meetings. Searching out my old friends, chasing after them. Telling them about Jesus.

Brenda and I started a meeting at a methadone clinic. Tomo Gilson was the manager. He was not a Christian himself, but recognising the change in me, he willingly opened the doors. One person came to our first meeting. No one to the next one. We wondered whether to give up but felt God prompting us to push through. Soon, there was a regular attendance of around twenty people and within a year, about sixty were gathering together at that clinic. At least ten of them found Christ that year. Sadly, many others only found death. Overdoses, murder and rape. It was a hard place to minister.

I chased down my old friend Martin and managed to get him into rehab. Within a week, he'd been changed radically. Changed by Jesus. It was such a thrilling moment. There was a glow about him; it was physically visible. So great was the change, I accidentally walked by him when I went to visit him a week or so later. To this day, Martin is continuing with his faith, now over in the UK.

We'd often do outreaches at the square right next to the big shopping centre in Tallaght. We'd give out tracts, we'd tell people about Jesus. Often just me and Brenda, with others gathering as they themselves got saved. I remember one day a young man went past. He must have been about twenty-five years old. I tried to give him a tract.

'Nah, you're alright pal, I'm not into that.'

'That's okay, then you're on your way to hell.'

'What d'ye mean?!'

'You're on your way to hell if you don't receive Jesus. If you're not into this, that's where you're going.'

As you can tell, I have a way with words.

'No one's ever told me that before. Give me that leaflet.'

It was around this time that I chased after Paddy Byrne. Paddy had been with me at school and had followed me out of the gates and into crime and drugs. Now he was living on the streets.

The thing is, if he saw me coming, he'd run the other way! I tell you, for a hopeless drug addict, he could run! This became a common occurrence, but I didn't give up.

'Paddy! Paddy! Stop! Let me talk to you!'

But he'd be gone, around the corner and over the fence. Anything other than talk to the Jesus freak.

I knew where he was sleeping, though. The car park of Aberlay Court Hotel, the very same place I used to shoot up cocaine. I took to visiting him at night – it was hard for him to run when he was in his sleeping bag! I'd leave food for him, along with notes from me, or sometimes a Christian tract. I'd try and speak to him and tell him that Jesus loved him. Not that he ever responded.

Chasing my old drug and crime friends was a common experience. Over the next few months, in fact, the years that followed, we have faithfully chased after and ministered to the people on the streets of Tallaght. We've seen healings, we've seen many come to Christ and by God's grace we've seen many come off heroin and cocaine.

There's a funny side to this, too. I would drive around, picking up my old drug addict pals, and throw them into the back of the van! The idea was to get them to a meeting and see the Holy Spirit do the rest. Not everyone appreciated this tactic and as I arrived on the various estates, I would see people scatter in all directions!

Through this time, though, local church remained tough. A theology that didn't welcome signs and wonders. And I didn't know how to handle that. There were occasions when they seemed to be saying things that just didn't line up with what I understood in the Bible. And I'm sad to say that when those occasions got too much, I regressed. Over a two-year period in Living Waters since my real salvation, I used drugs at least four times. It was usually as a reaction to things I was witnessing in the church that I just didn't agree with. I was too fiery. I was too immature. So immature that I slipped back.

That's when I found myself on a concrete slab in the middle of hell.

Anger

It was 2002 and I was angry. An angry young man, really. More pride in my passion for Jesus than understanding for others. Without the sense to manage the inconsistencies that come with any church.

For the most part, I was off drugs and everything looked to be about Jesus. It was all about Jesus, it had to be all about Jesus, and everybody had to be as fanatical as I was.

But I was so immature. *So* immature!

It was a good church. Living Waters. The pastors there were kind. They tried to help. But for me, it just wasn't radical enough. How could they condone some of the stuff that I saw on a Sunday? How could church be like this? It was like living half a Christian life, as far as I was concerned.

And of course, I had the answers. Oh yes, with my past, I had no hesitation in wading in. I would publicly argue with those around me. I had no hesitation in interrupting a meeting to point out the error of their ways.

The good people there were very accommodating. After a while they called it 'doing a Hammy'.

So immature. So full of pride. I saw what I thought was deception. I saw what I thought was compromise. And in some cases, I was right. There was some sin. Particularly regarding the lifestyle of one of the leaders. It wasn't addressed and it should have been.

But to wade in publicly with my 'holier than thou' comments, that was simply unacceptable.

My immaturity was on show for all to see. And just occasionally, everything got too much. I remember walking out of that church a number of times. And on four of those occasions over a two-year timeframe, I walked back in the direction of the drug dens that I knew so well.

'Hey Hammy, so good to see you.'

I had walked in the front door of one of the most renowned drug dens. I could smell the sweat, smell the drugs. I knew where I was, and I knew I shouldn't have been there.

'What have you got?'

'What do you want?'

I started to sniff cocaine. But that first time back in the drug den, it felt so bad. I knew I was wrong. Having paid for the drugs, I handed them back to Dunner the Dealer.

'No. You can have them. I can't do this.'

And with that I walked out.

It was pretty much the same again six months later. And again, after that.

But the fourth time was different.

From my point of view, church had been particularly bad that morning. Worship was half-hearted and the preach was all over the place, or so I thought. What was I doing there? How could this be called church?

As we walked out of the church building that morning, Brenda and I started an argument.

'Hammy, you simply can't do this. You explode at the slightest thing! You might even be right, but this isn't the way to do it.'

'Then what is the way?! I'm done with church! I've had enough. Why bother when there's so much compromise. The teaching this morning was appalling! And don't get me started on the worship!'

With that, I walked away. And down the road. Around the corner, in the direction of Bren's house. It was a Sunday lunchtime and I knew that they would be injecting. I went for speedballing that morning. Speedballing is taking heroin and cocaine together. Injecting both. A double hit.

And so, so stupid.

In the Middle of Hell

I was so angry I didn't care. I'd had enough. I didn't care what happened. For a moment in time, everything I had learned, everything I had read in the Bible, seemed irrelevant. My emotions were all over the place. I was angry with church. I was angry with Brenda for not agreeing with me. I was angry with God.

I felt the power of the drugs coursing through me. Heroin and cocaine together are an ungodly mix. And with my body being so unused to drugs, they were also a killer mix.

One of the ladies there called for an ambulance. I had begun to turn blue from the overdose. Unresponsive and in and out of consciousness, I somehow heard one of the crew shouting that she didn't think I was going to make it.

On the way to the hospital, the ambulance pulled over to the side of the road. I had gone into cardiac arrest and they were trying to resuscitate me.

I died three times in hospital over a period of one day. Each time, a defibrillator brought me back from the brink. The overdose was so intense and, with my body having no tolerance to drugs any more, none of the doctors thought I'd get through it.

That's when I woke up on a slab in the middle of hell.

On that fourth occasion of taking drugs – and on the third time I died that day, I found myself naked in the darkness, with a concrete slab underneath me. I felt its roughness, its coldness. I looked around but there was nothing to see. Pitch darkness.

I felt fear. Raw fear. I knew where I was. And I was afraid. Afraid in a way I had never felt before. I began to shake.

And then I heard the voices. There was a cackle in the blackness.

'Haha! Look at him! He trusted in Jesus and he's here with us!'

I started to scream.

'Jesus! Jesus! Help me!'

I just kept on shouting his name. Jesus. Jesus. Again and again, His name, shouted at the top of my voice.

The nurses tell me that I came round shouting 'Jesus'.

Later that day, the doctor who had been treating me came to see me. He was actually off duty, but came in, nevertheless.

The doctor told me that I had been dead for up to three to four minutes. I had caught pneumonia, caused by my lungs beginning to fill with fluid as I had died. Now in the resuscitation ward, I was looking up at the doctor's smiling face.

'I don't know how you're still here, Tommy. The machine was going crazy as we brought you back. Your heart was running so fast I thought it was literally going to explode! But you said something as you were coming through. You were shouting a name. Tommy, I'm telling you, stick close to that person.'

The whole thing was a sobering experience. My immaturity and anger at the church had got the better of me. I had been so very outspoken. And to be honest, I wasn't always right. Yes, sometimes the pastors may have been a bit misguided. And yes, there had even been compromise on occasion, but there's no excuse for the way I treated them, the way I spoke out publicly in meetings.

I felt Jesus' admonition for what I had done. It was a 'choose life or death' moment for me. I honestly believe this was a choice God was giving me at that moment. I felt God was saying, 'Tommy, you choose where you're going to end up.' I felt that if I continued, if I took drugs ever again, I really would end up on that cold concrete slab in the middle of a darkened hell.

Kingdom Faith

We were ten years or so at Living Waters. Involved in evangelism, helping to lead meetings, regularly attending. But the thing is, I had been so radically changed back at The Haven, I needed more than they could give.

During one of my early rehabs with Laurence, I had read that book by Colin Urquhart. He was someone who was totally radical, passionate about Jesus. That's where I could find help.

For the next five years I travelled over to Horsham, in England, twice a year for the leader's conference at Kingdom Faith, Colin's group of churches.

It was a life saver. It offered me the lifeline I needed, the teaching that I wanted. I began to learn some of the deeper things of the Christian faith. I found new relationships and received a lot of encouragement.

Strangely, something happened in that fifth year. The conference simply didn't feel as good. Something was missing. I kept it to myself, but it felt different. Whatever the reason, it just didn't feel the same.

It was the end of an era for me. In fact, even though I had said nothing, the next time I applied to join the leadership conference, I was advised that I was no longer invited. The person on the end of the phone was very polite but explained that they were changing their structures and could no longer work in the same way.

I loved my time with Colin and his team. They were so good to me, a lifeline when I needed it. I think they were simply planning to concentrate on their own churches and their own leaders, so it forced a change in me. I had to seek after God all the more. I had to find the life that I needed in God's word. And increasingly, I had to respond to what I felt was God's call on my own life.

New Church

For some time, I had been walking the streets of Kiltalown, one of the larger housing estates within Tallaght. There was another church in the area, and I didn't want to tread on their toes, but I felt an increasing call to this community, one of the darkest areas in Tallaght.

Things came to a head for me in a strange but perhaps typical way. Typical for me, anyway! I had a public stand-up argument with one of the leaders of Living Waters Church. I still believe that the man was making a number of accusations against me that were wrong, but typically for me, I did not respond well. I didn't actually hit him, but I was near to stepping back into my old fighting days at that moment! That was the day that Brenda and I walked out.

For the next couple of years, we visited a number of churches but were unable to settle. Increasingly I felt the call to Kiltalown, and the need to start a new church there. I walked the streets pretty much every day, praying.

I met the pastor of the church in that area on a few occasions, but the last time we met wasn't so good. A number of us had been gathering together as pastors in the area but as this included Catholics and one or two pastors who did not appear to believe in Jesus Christ, I raised the issue with the local pastor. I remember exactly where we were. McDonald's. Third table in on the left. Two coffees and two cheeseburgers.

'Alastair, how can we possibly continue to meet as a group of pastors when some of the lads don't even seem to have a proper faith?'

What happened next was remarkable. I have rarely seen people manifest demons publicly but honestly, that's exactly what happened. The pastor started screaming at me.

'How can you say that?! How dare you comment on the quality of another pastor's Christian life! What is it with you lot? You're always going on about the second coming but where is that coming? What are you going on about?!'

Without realising it, the pastor was quoting the Bible. 2 Peter 3, verses 3 and 4:

'Scoffers will come in the last days with scoffing, following their own sinful desires. They will say, "Where is the promise of his coming?"'

Interestingly, he went back to his church that next Sunday and resigned. The church closed. There were no longer any toes to tread on. Brenda and I could start a new church without conflict as soon as we had found a place to meet. There were so many people in need. So much need. An incredible amount of brokenness.

There was a lot to be done.

Chapter Nine

FIREBRAND

'Brenda do you really think we should be doing this?'

'God is saying it, isn't He?'

'Yes, I guess so. But it's such a massive thing. This is a big step for us.'

Location

But there was no getting away from it. I couldn't shake the conviction that we really should be starting a new church in Kiltalown. During those days I was continually walking around the estate, praying, calling on God for the salvation of the community, for a hand of rescue to those in chains, in pain, in despair. I felt led to walk into the local shop.

'Morning, Christy. Hey, I don't suppose you know whether there are any properties around here that could cope with us opening a church on Sundays? I really feel we need to start something, but I just don't know where to look.'

'What about over the road?'

'What do you mean?'

'The community centre, Hammy. I'm sure they'd be able to accommodate you.'

The thing is, in all the years that I had lived in the Tallaght area, I'd never noticed Kiltalown actually had a community centre. It had been there for years, but somehow, I had missed it. It was probably the drugs. Drugs do strange things to you. Some things you're very aware of, other things pass you by. Despite this community centre being less than 100 yards from where we used to live, I simply had no recollection of ever noticing it.

But there it was. Right in front of my eyes.

Firebrand Christian Church started in August 2013. There were three of us planning its launch. Me, Brenda and Eamon. Eamon was well into his seventies and joined us from the church we used to go to. He was a man on fire, desperate for the Holy Spirit to move and fully persuaded that he should be part of this new venture.

Our name was thought through. Firebrand Christian Church. All three of us had caught fire. And we were desperate for the streets of Kiltalown to burn with the good news of Jesus Christ and for the work of the Holy Spirit to be so evident, He could not be ignored. It was the 18th Century evangelist John Wesley who said, 'Get on fire for God and men will come and see you burn.' That was us.

The reference in the Bible we were thinking of as we named the church is from Amos. This is what it says:

'You were like a firebrand plucked from the burning.' (NKJV)

And that's my story, really. A firebrand plucked from burning. I should by all reasonable accounts be dead. Shot. Stabbed.

Overdosed. Death had been all around me. But God had other plans. He's made me a firebrand, rescued from the burning.

Not only is it my story, it's our mission. Firebrand Church has a calling to pluck people from the very fires of hell. We know what it is to live in hell, and we know what it is to be plucked from hell. We are the rescued. We are the saved. And we plan to rescue and save as many as we can while we still live and breathe. We are the burning ones, burning with a passion for Christ. And by God's grace, the fire will spread.

In order to get into the community centre that very first day of church, we had to cross a Garda taped off area. There had been a murder the night before on the steps of the centre. A challenging start for a new church to say the least!

That first Sunday, we managed eight in total. Me, Brenda, and Eamon. A local evangelist joined us. Then there were our three boys and Nicole, the girlfriend of one of our lads. Their relationship didn't last long, but Nicole stayed with us and was a real help in those early days.

We started inviting the local kids to join us and set up a Sunday School, which Nicole ran for us. She was only sixteen and a very young Christian but nevertheless this seemed to have an effect on the crazy kids that we saw around the streets of Kiltalown.

The murder the night before on the steps of the centre seemed to have an effect on our evangelist friend. Despite committing to join us, that first meeting was also his last. It's a tough area.

We did our own evangelism, though, often outside the centre and across the road by the shops. It was hard. It felt hard to break through in praise and worship. Perhaps not a surprise when you consider the spiritual darkness of the area. But we pushed through anyway.

Not that there were many people turning up on Sunday as a result of those early outreaches.

Jonathan

'Hammy, I really think we should go to this conference! It's in Wolverhampton – led by a guy called Steve Uppal. He's got this speaker that I would really like to hear.'

And so it was that Brenda and I, along with Eamon, found ourselves at a church leaders conference in Wolverhampton in 2015.

At this point, I have to come clean. I really did not like the headline speaker that Brenda was fond of. I found him over the top and was uncomfortable with his approach to ministry. It may have been me, of course. I feel God has cleared out a lot of religious rubbish over the years but maybe there was a bit hanging on still.

The main speaker did his thing. I sat there. But then something happened that totally changed me.

Steve Uppal introduced the next speaker – someone called Jonathan Conrathe. Jonathan leads an evangelistic organisation called Mission24, but I'd not heard of him or the organisation before.

The moment Jon began to speak, I knew that God was doing a number on me through every word. The detail of the talk is lost to me now but what I remember were the powerful testimonies that he shared throughout his talk. People being healed, deaf ears opened, blind eye seeing, and the dead being raised. This was New Testament Church Christianity. This was what I longed for and here I was witnessing the fact that God still did these things. Not only that, but the guy was also a Brit! God was working through someone that seemed very English, very normal, almost understated.

Unpersuaded

Despite the encouragement from visiting Wolverhampton, things didn't change at home base. I was considering closing the church, simply because no one was coming.

'Lord, I'm not convinced. I think this must just be me.'

Some weeks, I was preaching just to Brenda. Other weeks, she was preaching just to me. And that was it! If Eamon was there, then there were three of us. If the kids and Nicole came then we made it to seven. No growth and seven people is not a church.

And then, dear Eamon died. He was our encourager, our champion. We so miss him.

We pushed on. We would regularly set up the room for a full attendance. We were persistent in our prayers. But nothing happened. And there we were, me preaching to Brenda and Brenda preaching to me.

So, on this particular Saturday night, I'd had enough. I had laid out my complaints before the Lord and had determined in my own mind that it really hadn't been God's intention to start Firebrand Church at all. It had simply been a figment of my imagination, a reflection of me not having been happy in the previous church.

I decided to do one more thing. One more fleece laid before the Lord.

'God, if no one else turns up tomorrow, then that is it. I'll take it as a sign from you that we really shouldn't have started this venture. We'll go off and find ourselves a good church and work out our faith in other ways.'

I really didn't expect anyone through the door that Sunday morning. Why should anyone come? After all, no one had come through the door for weeks!

'Hey Hammy, it's good to see you.'

I looked up in disbelief as Milo walked into the building. Originally a professional boxer, he lost it all to crack cocaine. We had chatted over previous weeks and I had challenged him to ask God to change his life.

And there he was. That Sunday. The very time I had asked God for a clear direction on the future of the church. The very time that I had considered closing the doors for good.

I asked Milo how come he had turned up.

'Hammy, it was really strange! I woke up at three o'clock this morning. I just felt compelled to come. I haven't thought about you, I hadn't thought about church. But there it was. I was wide awake in the middle of the night and knowing that I had to go to church today. I couldn't remember where you said to meet, but when I woke up, I found a card you'd given me. So here I am.'

As we finished our conversation, I looked up and in front of me was Sandra. Sandra was Eamon's daughter. She explained that in the middle of the night she had also been woken up and felt that God was telling her to come to our church.

At that moment, it felt like we had a church of six thousand rather than six. We were overjoyed, we never gave up and I can honestly say that if you know God has called you to do something, keep going, don't give up on it. Jesus will bring you through regardless of how you are feeling. Stand your ground!

I well and truly got the message.

It was still hard, though, with our growth up and down each week and occasionally I really was just preaching to Brenda.

'Hammy, we need to push through. What about inviting Jonathan Conrathe? That could change things for us.'

'Honey, he won't come. Of course he won't! How many of us are attending on an average Sunday? You, me and Nicole! At best we get to ten. Fifteen is the most we've had. Why should an evangelist with a worldwide ministry be interested in that?'

'We can but ask ...'

And so we did.

He came.

That Friday night, our meeting was full. We were a church of maybe fifteen people at the time. 110 people turned up to that meeting. Pretty much every chair was taken. We were using a bigger community centre and had worked hard to get the news out that Jonathan would be speaking and that there would be healing and miracles. We followed this up on the Saturday with outreaches on the street and then on the Sunday, Jonathan spoke to our church.

The thing is, on the Sunday we were back to just the regular crowd. Nevertheless, Jon spoke powerfully and there is no doubt that our church was blessed.

Television Cameras

It was as we were leaving the building that Jon suddenly stopped, turned around and looked back across the meeting space.

'Tommy, I see television cameras over in that corner of the room! I do! I see television cameras in here recording what's happening. I believe God is saying something prophetically to you.'

I shrugged it off. To be honest, I thought Jonathan was off his head! How could that ever happen? A congregation of ten to fifteen people on some back of beyond housing estate to the south of Dublin.

Three weeks later the phone call came through.

'Hello, this is TV3. We were wondering if it would be possible to film your church? We're making a set of documentaries reflecting some of the harder edged communities within Ireland. Somebody was telling us about you and how you're working hard to change the environment in Jobestown and Kiltalown. I wonder, could we film you?'

And so it began. TV3, one of Ireland's main television companies, followed us around with cameras for almost a year. The cameras were set up on Sundays – and on the exact spot that Jon had seen prophetically.

Second Visit

Jonathan Conrathe has visited us a number of times now. It was on the second visit that a pretty lady called Shirley came into the meeting. At the end, she came to the front and prayed for God to change her life.

That night, she went home to tell her partner. At the time, we were unaware of the connection – her partner was Paddy Byrne, the school friend that would do anything he could to run away from me talking to him! By now, Paddy had been through detox and had turned his life around.

As Shirley shared her faith, Paddy began to frown.

'This is real, isn't it? I'm going to go there tomorrow.'

So, in the end, Paddy chased after me! We talked at length.

'Hammy, I really have turned my life around. Detox worked for me. I have a beautiful partner, a house, a great job. I should be happy. But I'm not. There's something missing. And I'm forever looking over my shoulder. What if the drugs take hold again? I wake up thinking of drugs every day. I'm so fearful of returning to my old life. But I'm looking at you – and you have something I haven't got. What's the story?'

'Paddy, I have the thing that will stop you thinking of drugs every day. The Bible says he whom the son sets free is free indeed.'

And there we were. Paddy was no longer running. I had the privilege of leading him to a faith in Christ and, a couple of years later, I had the additional privilege of officiating at the marriage of Paddy and Shirley. Today they are leaders in the church.

To date, fourteen of Shirley's relatives have come to church as a result of Paddy and Shirley's faith. All have found their own faith in Christ.

That second visit from Jonathan was special for another reason. As well as many Christian salvations, we saw a number of healings and miracles. Many people felt an overpowering presence of the Holy Spirit and were lying on the floor, unable to get up, some lying still, others crying and shaking. At the meetings, Paul Gibbons witnessed a cancerous lump on his neck disappear. The hospital has since confirmed there are no cancerous cells left in his body.

Paula is another with a story to tell. When her husband Larry (one of my employees) gave his life to Jesus, she ridiculed him. She came to one of the early Jonathan Conrathe meetings, sat at the back and laughed at us. But the Holy Spirit had other ideas. That night she found a faith in Christ and was baptised in the Holy Spirit, speaking in tongues, laughing with joy.

Paula had been an orphan. The nuns at the orphanage had sold her on to the pharmaceutical companies for experiments. She couldn't remember much about it, except for a mark on her neck and the fact she could not sleep lying down because of breathing problems. Nor could she eat solids because of a swallowing problem. With Jonathan and the church praying for Paula, she went home and was able to sleep lying down without any issues. The next day, she was able to eat solids with no swallowing problems. God saved her and healed her at the same time.

Suzanne

I woke one day with a Holy Spirit prompt to go and find Suzanne. Suzanne was a friend going back to our school days. We'd seen her around over the years and, like so many, she had become caught up in the drug culture.

It was definitely a God-prompted moment. When I arrived at Suzanne's house, she was there with her mother and brother. Her brother was well known as a gangster and armed robber. I spoke to all three about the Lord and turning their life around.

Two nights later, Suzanne's brother showed up at an outreach event we were holding.

'Hey, good to see you here, Connor. What's brought you here?'

'Well, I heard that you have something here, so I thought I'd give robbing a break.'

That night he prayed and asked Jesus to change his life. Two weeks later, he was dead. God's timing is perfect.

I continued to talk to Suzanne.

'Suzanne, if you put your faith in Jesus, He will deliver you and set you free instantly. God is no respecter of people – look, He did it for me! He can do the same for you.'

Suzanne decided to give it a go. She came to live at our place as she came off drugs. I remember her coming out for a drive with us on her first night, her head out of the window as she was sick. The cold turkey was tough.

'Hammy, you absolute scumbag! You said it would be easy!'

That evening, Brenda and I prayed with her as she went to bed. As her head hit the pillow, she encountered Jesus in the most beautiful way. As she was listening to a worship CD, Jesus met with her. She had never felt His presence like that before. Filled with love and overcome with the presence of the Holy Spirit, she was pinned to the bed as God ministered to her.

That night, Suzanne was instantly delivered from heroin, methadone, various tablets and alcohol. Suzanne had been addicted from an early age. God met her that day, and as the Bible says, He 'redeemed the years the locusts had eaten.'

Suzanne had a glorious new faith. She took her children to school – the first time she had bothered about their education. Complete with a Bible under her arm, she walked into the school building. The headmaster saw her and burst into tears, unable to control his weeping. Suzanne was so visibly different, he hardly recognised her. The local dentist agreed to sort out Suzanne's teeth, damaged as they were by drugs and neglect. The dentist, too, was amazed at the change and offered to do the work for free.

Suzanne died on Christmas day a couple of years later from a heart attack. Her daughter Megan and her other brother (also a former bank robber) are in church with us today. The brother has retrained and is now a qualified criminologist (the humour is not lost on me!). Suzanne's mother also came to church and was miraculously cured of cancer, following prayer.

As I look back at those moments with Suzanne, I have no doubt at all that God is able to redeem the most lost and most damaged lives. That's my story, of course. That's Suzanne's story.

Miraculous

We began to see God moving in the same miraculous ways that we had witnessed with Jonathan, and people were coming as a result. Our congregation of fifteen quickly grew to fifty. We moved to a school to accommodate the increase, and then again to a larger school. Each week we were seeing the Holy Spirit move miraculously in the meetings. Sometimes with healing, often with demonic manifestations and a complete release for the individuals involved.

I remember being a bit sceptical about deliverance ministry. Could people really have demons? I remember reading about it in Luke's gospel one afternoon, and that very same evening having to confront a couple in the meeting who were clearly manifesting something ungodly. It's as if God had intervened with that scripture at the very moment that we needed it.

Jonathan has helped us there as well. He's taken most of the church through the Mission24 Impact Course. That has been so helpful to us, and very practical in dealing in the areas of deliverance, healing and miracles.

The church has become quite a prayer centre as well. We meet once a week to pray and there is such a spiritual heat on those meetings. One woman felt to come along to these meetings, having read something about Jesus' return in the Bible. She was just a normal, every-day, stay-at-home mum, but in reading the Bible, God had begun to work in her life. She asked Jesus to change her life that very next Sunday. I remember her being unable to stop crying. Today she is part of our congregation. It wasn't long afterwards that she brought her boyfriend and daughter along. Matthew, her boyfriend, was deeply affected by the meeting. He started to read the Bible, finishing the gospels within a few days.

On another occasion, prayers were answered in a very special way, and I had the privilege of leading my ma to Christ just a few weeks before she died.

Where we meet to pray is interesting. It's on the top story of a building on the side of Tallaght Mountain. Remember me telling you about that? It's a place used in witchcraft. We've had our battles as we stand together for Tallaght, but we are slowly seeing the clouds push back. The mountain is not used so often for ceremonies and there are not so many black magic shrines anymore. We continue to pray this will have an effect on Tallaght as a whole, with less murders and suicides.

Mountain Challenges

There's still a battle for the town, though, and the mountain is central to that. One time I was doing some outdoor preaching there and was attacked. A broken leg was the result. But there is no doubt the Holy Spirit is also at work. In that same preach, I saw the demons on the hillside being scattered as the word of God was declared.

There are a few shops at the bottom of the mountain, and I was waiting there one day when a beautiful woman began to walk towards me. She looked like a top model – perfect features. As she approached, if felt like she was looking right into my soul. It felt as though I was being pulled towards her. As she approached my face, she changed. She became a wolf, and then, growling at me, she disappeared.

I need to tell you that the story you have just read really happened. It wasn't a dream. I was standing outside a shop, waiting for family. It actually happened. Demons are real.

I do have dreams as well, though. On one occasion I woke from a particularly vivid dream. In the dream, I had been speaking over Tallaght. I had been declaring over the town, God's freedom. I shouted:

'I release you in the name of Jesus.'

I waited. But nothing happened. In the dream, I asked God why there was no result. Then I saw a black cat go past me. It looked at me with yellow eyes.

In the morning I shared this with Brenda and we looked up 'cat with yellow eyes' on a search engine, as we both thought that cats generally had green eyes. What came up on Google was very revealing. There are breeds of cat with yellow eyes but a black cat with yellow eyes is synonymous with witchcraft and death – and a number of the sites that came up were related to witchcraft.

Apostolic

We have been so blessed by Jonathan Conrathe's visits. He has become a close friend, and he blessed us in another way as well. At that first weekend with Jonathan, he suggested that we needed some help. As a result, Jonathan put us in touch with the Four12 Global apostolic movement. We've been partners with them ever since. Just to have encouragement and input from people like Andrew Selley in South Africa and Jonathan Stanfield in the Isle of Man has made an incredible difference to us. As leaders, Brenda and I are in a better place because of it. We've learned what New Testament Christianity is about, how we can structure church, how we can best operate in the community around us. As a church, we have a broader vision, an awareness of what God is doing in the rest of the world, and all that can therefore be applied to a housing estate in Dublin. He is the same God, the same Holy Spirit. What God does in other parts of the world can be applied in the same way to us. To a place that others may have forgotten – but God has not.

Today, there are about 120 of us. People come from all over Tallaght and some from further afield. Over the years we've seen thousands come through our doors, often receiving salvation and healing, and leaving totally different as a result. With help from Four12, we have teams joining us on a regular basis – and we even have friends from South Africa who have stayed beyond team and joined us in our long-term mission.

We have seen favour from the local council as well in helping us find Sunday meeting accommodation. The local Garda recommended us to the council on the basis of the number of people that were coming out of drug addiction and the corresponding reduction in local crime.

We continue to grow as a church family. Most in Tallaght know about us – it's hard not to, as we are still on the streets most weekends, speaking about Jesus and seeing people find a faith in Christ, along with healing for their bodies.

Chapter Ten

CHANGING

As we grow as a church, it's fair to say that I've changed too. By God's grace, I learned not to be so blunt, nor to take offence when I see something that speaks of religion rather than real faith. As He does for all of us, God takes us on a journey and only shows things up in our lives as and when we are ready to deal with them.

The Prophetess

I was at a Four12 conference on the occasion that the guest speaker was a well-known prophetess. She spoke regularly on the prophetic and with a good deal of accuracy. But as I listened to her, I just couldn't accept what she was saying. I found myself wanting to disagree with her. I felt so uncomfortable. It reminded me of the time we had been over to Wolverhampton and had first met Jonathan Conrathe. The main speaker then had been someone Brenda really liked, but I had struggled to the point of almost leaving the meeting. And here I was again, displaying the same behaviour.

I heard a voice as I listened to her, along the lines of, 'Don't listen to this woman! Don't let her pray for you.'

As we moved into a ministry time at the end of the talk, I was determined not to respond. At one point, the response was so obviously for all of us, I thought it might look odd if I didn't put my hand up.

As my hand went up, it was as if a bolt of lightning struck it. I was thrown back through the air a good number of feet, almost hovering above the ground as I flew. I landed on the feet of Andrew Selley, the main apostle for Four12.

For the next hour or so, I felt completely bathed in the Holy Spirit. It was like I was under a waterfall. There were times when the presence of God was so intense, I was crying out to Him to stop it! But He didn't stop, and I came up off that floor a different person.

God dealt with a religious spirit within me in that meeting. I felt free. For most of my life, I had suffered with a mild pain or pressure on the right-hand side of my forehead. As I got up, I noticed it had gone. And it has not returned.

God dealt with something else as well, while I lay on the floor. Many years previously, an old pastor had spoken over me, saying I would never be a good pastor and that I wasn't even a good evangelist. Unknowingly, the curse of those words had remained with me and affected me. But now I was free.

Upon our return to Tallaght, something was different. I had a newfound certainty that God had good plans for us as a church, I found I had a better ability to preach and minister. And the church began to grow.

Changed Lives

Come with me, let me invite you to one of our Sunday meetings . . . We're at a bigger school nowadays, with a congregation of 120 or so. As we arrive early, you'll see quite a few people already here. There's Paddy and his friend PJ. Nicole is here. Eamon is with the Lord now, of course, but that's his brother-in-law Jimmie, over there. Such a lovely man with a beautiful spirit; he's a great encourager.

Come inside. Let me introduce you to a few of my friends.

You may remember Nicole. She was our very first church member and spent the first few months watching me preach to Brenda and Brenda preach to me. She ran the children's ministry – and still does. Such faithfulness. The only difference: there are so many children now, Nicole can no longer remember all their names. Nicole will tell you some fun stories from those early days. Like the time the children gave her a can of Lucozade . . .

'Aw, thanks, you guys, but you really shouldn't have. You can't really afford to be buying me presents.'

'Oh, we didn't buy it, miss.'

'What do you mean? You didn't steal it, did you?'

'But don't you like Lucozade, miss?'

We're a few years on now, but typically Nicole is dealing weekly with the same kind of issues as children from the local estates find out what it is to live God's way.

Paddy Byrne is here, too. He may well have welcomed you in the car park as you arrived, or maybe he's at the welcome table. Free from drugs, happily married and part of our leadership team, his journey has mirrored my own to a degree.

'I followed Hammy into the gangs,' says Paddy. 'Our Friday night fun was watching cars get stolen and run into the ground. That was our movies. There was nothing else to do on the streets. I'm so glad to have had Hammy chase after me and introduce me to Jesus. Many of our gang friends from those early days were not so fortunate. Most came to an early grave.'

Healed Marriage

Mark, a particularly accomplished guitarist, is leading worship today. Originally from Tallaght, he and Lorraine travel in each week to be part of us. A few years back, Mark was in church and in tears. Lorraine had said she was going to leave him and was packing her bags that morning. She didn't have a Christian faith and felt drained by the marriage. Mark and I prayed together, and I left it at that at the time.

That afternoon, I had a call about a van I was hoping to buy. It had to be a specific variety in order to help with church and outreaches and I'd not been able to find one anywhere. The tip-off came that this very van was for sale quite locally. I drove out to see it and realised that the person selling the van was just a few doors away from Mark and Lorraine, so I called in.

The couple were about to go their separate ways. As I sat in their kitchen, I felt a boldness of the Holy Spirit to speak into the situation.

'Lorraine, you're broken. Jesus needs to heal you.'

Within a moment, Lorraine was in tears. I saw the Holy Spirit ministering to her, so obviously touching her life. Later that day, Mark led her to the Lord. Subsequently, Lorraine was healed of a significant back condition which could have left her in a wheelchair. Today Mark and Lorraine help us lead Firebrand Church.

I love God's timing in all of this. At the very moment Lorraine was about to leave, God sent me there. He's never late, always on time. And he's the best secretary in the world – there's no way I could organise a diary in the way He does!

Lives on Fire

Nicole remembers a prophecy over the church. God calls us all the 'burning ones'. It's true. Sometimes, when you have been forgiven much, you burn brighter. That's true of Michelle, sitting on the front row on this particular Sunday. A former crack addict, she was delivered from many demonic influences and healed of arthritis at one memorable prayer meeting. Gina is next to her, faithfully supporting and discipling.

There's another lady next to Michelle and Gina. She has a story as well. Healed of arthritis too, with a doctor's confirmation that meds are no longer required. She was healed from a lump on her wrist recently – we all saw as the lump disappeared in front of our eyes.

Next to these ladies is a younger girl. She's off smoking weed now and has been signed off by the psychiatrist with no further psychosis apparent.

Changed lives. Lives on fire. As we worship this particular morning, look around with me. Each face, each voice reflecting Jesus. Trophies of grace.

Dermo's there at the back, welcoming latecomers. We are seeing a lot of people just turn up on a Sunday nowadays, having heard of what God is doing with us. There's Ross and Leah, a young couple helping us so much with church life. Ross was a declared atheist. Jesus sorted that one out! The sound is being managed by Glen this morning while his wife Marilee is in the worship band. They're from Cape Town. Both readily admit this is a very different church and calling to their home church in South Africa. But they know that they would be nowhere else.

Julie is helping with vocals in the band today. She's just in from Brazil. We really are becoming international. To the side there's PJ. He was here early as well, putting the chairs out. PJ has had the joy of seeing nearly all his close relatives coming to faith in Christ in our church.

We break bread together this morning. There's Avril, another of our leaders, helping to distribute the bread and wine.

Another lady comes to the microphone to share. She's comparatively new.

'I want you to know that speaking like this was one of my greatest fears. But I've chosen to walk out of the darkness and into the light. If you live in darkness, you live in lies. When you're in the light, you're in God's territory and He's there to help you with every fear. It's a choice – light or darkness. Live in the light.'

Worship

Our worship is pretty raw. There's a wildness to the singing. We've all been forgiven so much, our thanksgiving and worship overflows with the realisation. So many of us would be a Garda statistic were it not for God's intervention.

As we start to worship on this particular Sunday, you can see Mark lead us in a song that is fairly new to us. It speaks of us bringing all our failures and all our addictions to the foot of the cross. These are strong words for our congregation. So many have come out of a gangster culture, one laced with drugs and alcohol.

I follow through on the theme of the worship as I preach that morning. The goodness of God. Our willing sacrifice to Him because He sacrificed all for us. Psalm 16 says, 'You are my Lord; I have no God apart from you.' How true for each of us. And as we reach out, He reaches us.

I say: 'If you are in this place and you have a broken heart this morning, Jesus can heal it.'

I explain that outside of God there are storms. But we can be inside. We can know Jesus as our rock.

I appeal for anyone needing to know Jesus as saviour to come forward.

'If you are broken this morning, you are in good company. We've all been broken. But we've been mended. Come this morning, come out of fear, away from oppression, out of addiction. Come to Jesus.'

As the meeting closes, eight people come forward to be saved. Among them are members of a notorious gangster family. By God's grace, these stories are a regular occurrence in Firebrand Church.

Still Changing

Thanks for being with me on this particular Sunday morning; I hope you enjoyed the virtual visit. We've been changed and we are changing still as a church. It's true for all of us, of course. It's what the Bible calls being 'sanctified'. God changed us in the moment we met Him, but our lives continue to get changed from one degree to the next.

'And we all, with unveiled face, beholding the glory of the Lord, are being transformed into the same image from one degree of glory to another.' (2 Corinthians 3: 18)

We are being saved and we are saved. We've all been saved from so much. And all that Jesus has saved us from – well, we won't know the extent of it in this life!

Chapter Eleven

I SPEAK TO DEAD PEOPLE

I see dead people and I speak to them every day. God keeps introducing me to them. People without hope, without life. Zombie-like, they walk the streets of Tallaght, fixing their next high. Captive to heroin or cocaine. Caught in a spiral of debt. Lost to the street corners where prostitution sells itself. Alone, lifeless.

The Bible says that we are all dead in our sins:

'And you were dead in the trespasses and sins in which you once walked, following the course of this world, following the prince of the power of the air, the spirit that is now at work.' (Ephesians 2:1-2)

There's the truth. Anyone outside of a faith relationship with Christ is dead. It's just that on the streets of Dublin, we know it: we see it played out graphically on every corner, in so many houses, drug dens and brothels.

'I'm Home'

I remember one Sunday a man appearing at the back of the meeting just as I was concluding my preach. It had been a simple talk that morning – repent or perish. I was just at that altar call moment, inviting anyone who needed Christ to come to the front of the meeting.

'No matter what you have done in your life, no matter what you have done, if you truly repent, Jesus will forgive you and save you.'

Within moments, the man at the back was running forward. He flung himself into my arms, tears in his eyes. 'I'm home,' he whispered. 'I'm home.'

I had not seen him before. I had no idea who he was. It turns out he was a hitman. A murderer. And he was dying from kidney failure.

As his whole body shook that morning, he prayed his way into the Kingdom of God:

'Lord Jesus, I am so sorry for living my life my own way. Please forgive me for trying to live without You. Please forgive me for all I have done wrong. I ask You to come into my life right now. Please come into my life and fill me with the Holy Spirit. I receive You and I thank You for what You have done.'

If you're reading this and you have never prayed a prayer like that, now's your time. Pray it out – and tell someone with a Christian faith what you have done. No matter what you have done in your life, come truly repentant and Jesus really will forgive you.

'Go and Speak to Him'

Another time, I was having a cup of tea and a catch up with the local Methodist minister. As I looked out of his rectory window, I saw a young man going by. We had chatted before. I felt God tell me to go and speak to him and that I should do it straight away.

'Hey! Grady! Come here to me for a minute. I want to talk to you. I want to tell you about Jesus.'

He laughed at me.

'What are you saying? What are you looking for?'

'I want to tell you about Jesus. You need to give your life to Him.'

'What do I do, Hammy?'

'You give up your way of life. You give your life to Him.'

'What does that look like?'

'You break into people's houses. You steal from them. Ask forgiveness. Ask God to change your life and He will.'

'But what would I do for money?'

'You do the same as the rest of us. You get a job. You'd work for a living.'

'You must be joking! I'm not giving up my robbing for anybody!'

It was four o'clock on a Friday afternoon when that happened. At six o'clock that night, Grady was brutally murdered by a local gang. They had found him breaking into some premises they owned. In full view of everyone on the main road, they attacked him with knives and machetes. According to the public, it took him a long time to die. My prayer is that in the conversation we had, even as he was dying, he was seeking forgiveness and finding Jesus Christ. I fully believe that one day I will see him again in glory.

Forgiven

One day a man came to church with a girl on his arm. At the end of the meeting, he sought me out.

'Tommy, I need to be forgiven.'

'For what?'

'My girl. She's had an abortion. I want to ask forgiveness for that. I was part of it. I was part of the decision. It haunts me.'

As I prayed for him, I felt the fire of God go through him. He was shaking uncontrollably.

That man was dead within a week. He mistakenly overdosed on sleeping tablets.

You've met Milo. He was the guy who was woken up at 3:00am, feeling God had told him to come along to our church meeting. It didn't completely change him, but I knew he had a faith.

Milo was homeless most of the time, but we all loved him, cared for him in any way we could. He was even filmed by the TV cameras for that documentary. At that time, he had just come out of hospital, having had pneumonia. He described to the cameras how Jesus had met him in hospital. At the end of the interview, he said this:

'I don't know what's going to happen in my life but there is something that I know for sure – whenever I go, I'm going to be with Jesus.'

That was on the Sunday. On the Monday he died of an overdose.

Business Again

I think I'd say that one of my strongest giftings is as an evangelist. As I've continued with my own small company, I've made use of the opportunities that this gives me to share Jesus.

The way I started up in business again, after being free from drugs, is itself quite a story. Following that help from Laurence, and having been completely set free, I immersed myself in God's word for almost a year. During that time, Brenda and I saw finances arrive supernaturally. We were never without enough cash to buy food. However, one of the ways we received finance was through social welfare. One time, the cheque simply didn't arrive. I didn't have the money for the bus fare so had to walk over to the offices.

It was while I was waiting in the queue at the social welfare offices that it began to dawn on me. What I was doing was simply not a good witness. I could overhear others in the queue talking about different ways in which they were trying to defraud the government, using the various social welfare schemes available.

'Lord, this is honestly not giving glory to You. It seems to me I'm begging off the government. I'm not going to do this. God I'm going to trust You. I'm going to trust that You get me a job instead of having to queue for money that I shouldn't really be accepting.'

And with that, I left the queue and walked home.

I arrived back home to a phone call from the council.

'Mr Hanrahan, I've been trying to reach you for ages. I've been looking for your phone number for the last six months! But suddenly it's appeared on my table. I'm not sure how it's got here but I have fourteen jobs for you – are you interested?'

Within a few days, there had been a phone call from another council. In this case, it was from a different part of the country – a place I had never worked.

'I don't know who you are, but your name and phone number are on a piece of paper on my desk. I'm not quite sure how it got there but I wonder whether you'd be interested in some work? Can you call in to discuss it?'

During those first few weeks of the new business, I learned again and again what it means to trust God and to put Him first. As I stepped out of the Social Security office, God stepped into my bank account.

The Shower and the Roof

The council called me in to fix a leak in a shower that had recently been fitted. While I was there, I talked to the young lady in the house, sharing my Christian faith.

A week later, the leak was back. And a week after that, it started again. The contractor was concerned that I couldn't seem to fix it. The thing is, it seemed impossible to me that there still was a leak.

It was on that fourth visit that I met the young lady's brother. The previous evening, he had tried to commit suicide. As the three of us talked, I had the privilege of leading both of them to a faith in Jesus. What I hadn't realised from my earlier visits was that the young lady's child had cancer behind the eye. She and her brother asked me to pray for the child. I remember praying and using the words 'unspecified cancer' as I prayed. It was an odd use of words and not part of my normal vocabulary.

I heard from the young lady a few days later when she called me.

'I wanted to tell you that the tests are through. My daughter is completely healed. There is no sign of the cancer! The funny thing is, the consultant has called it an 'unspecified cancer' on his notes. That's what he said. I remember that's exactly what you prayed.'

Another time, I had helped fit some fibreglass roofing. This type of roofing is seamless and does not leak. However, every time it rained in this particular case, there was a leak. Four times I was called out and four times I tried to fix it. I couldn't understand how the leak was happening and actually offered the money back on the job. On that fourth time, as I was coming down the ladder, I slipped slightly and was rescued by one of the site workers. It was a strange thing. Normally I would have simply said 'thank you'. But on this occasion, I started by saying 'I'm a Christian'.

The young man who looked at me was taken aback.

'That's really funny, you saying that. I was thinking just this morning what a born-again Christian might be. Do you mind if we talk some more?'

We shared breakfast together in his van and I had the privilege of leading him to Christ.

The roof never leaked again.

The Neighbour

One of the specialisms of my company relates to reinventing ordinary bathrooms as disability bathrooms. Over the years, I found that many of the people I talk to are more than willing to listen to the gospel. They've been disabled or they have a severe illness, and this makes them more open to me being able to share with them the joy of who Jesus Christ is.

I had been working on a particular house. The man I was working for was really rather inhospitable and it was the neighbour, Alan, who invited me over for a cup of tea. I spoke about my faith but didn't get a response.

Three years later, the council called me back and I recognised the address – it was where Alan lived. As soon as I arrived, I could see he was not well. It was clear I was converting the bathroom into a disability unit for someone who didn't have long to live.

'Alan, it seems to me you really don't have long. You remember me telling you about Jesus?'

That morning, I introduced Alan to his saviour. Two weeks later he was with Him in paradise.

The stories are many. The time I helped a lady into the house with her shopping, introducing her to Jesus and then learning that she had terminal cancer. She died two weeks later, trusting her Saviour.

I had some work with a contractor. The day I chose to be on site was one of the hottest days of the year and I had the job of carrying materials from the ground floor up to the top of an apartment building, five floors higher. Some of the pieces I was carrying were simply too awkward for one man to handle. There was a young labourer on site, and I asked if he would be willing give me a hand. He was happy to do so.

The work ended with the two of us sitting on the top of the roof looking out over the housing complex. I learned that the young man was nineteen years old and a trainee engineer. In fact, he was only on site for that one day. A few minutes later, we were both kneeling on the roof of that building as he prayed a prayer and asked Jesus to change his life.

As we finished praying, I saw that there were tears in the young man's eyes.

'Can I tell you a story, Hammy? The reason I wanted to pray just now – the reason I was so keen to find out about Jesus is because of my friend. She was one of my best friends and a week ago she died of leukaemia. I was with her when she went. Honestly, I have never seen so much joy in any one person as I saw on her face at that moment. As she was dying, she reached out her hand to me. She looked up and pointed. "Look," she said, "He's coming! He's coming for me!" Hammy, she died with a smile on her face. What you told me today confirms it for me. What she saw was real. And now I've got it too. Thank you. Thank you so much.'

A Long Journey

As I look back at my past, as I think of the more recent times and the lives that have been changed, it seems like a different world.

The Hammy that inhabited the gangs is gone. What was I thinking, to have even considered that road? The thing is, I was impressionable, and to be frank, gangs is about all I knew. Slowly I was drawn into that lifestyle, and with it, the drugs.

As a comparatively young man, I liked what I saw with the Northies. They looked the real thing. They weren't, of course. When I look at that time now, I see lazy men who hadn't done a day's work in their lives, drinking heavily and hanging around outside the bookies shops most of the time. Living off others, cruelly using others to their own ends, wrapping it in politics and declaring it was fine to kill in their name.

By God's grace, I'm different today. Reflective of our church name, Jonathan Conrathe prophesied over us one time, reminding us that we are on fire because He has caused the fire within us. And that the fire will spread, it will reach into Dublin itself, it will change our city. And beyond as well. Thorough our relationship with Four12, we are seeing nations changed. That we have a part to play in that is entirely down to God's goodness.

Always Yes

I want to end with a particular story. You may not remember Alice. She comes into this story pretty early on. She was my ma's friend, the babysitter. The lady that abused me in my own home.

The day she walked into church, my emotions were all over the place. I hadn't seen her in all these years and there she was. What to do? How to react?

At that moment, it all came flooding back. All the years came together in a moment of time as Alice walked in. Ma hitting me. Da's drinking. My sister dying. The Christian Brothers. The attempts on my life. The stealing, the crimes. The heroin, the cocaine.

It was overwhelming. My whole life was being paraded in front of me. All the hurt and abuse. All the things I had done. My crimes, my stupidity. Everything was on show, played out in my mind at that moment.

Part of me wanted to go over and throw Alice out of the building. But I chose to do nothing and simply pray.

At the end of the morning, she was the first one to the front, the first one saying a prayer of repentance. Asking forgiveness for her past and inviting Jesus into her life.

I chose to forgive her. I chose to celebrate with her the new life that she had received. And just as she received mercy, so for every one of us.

We all have that opportunity. For every one of us, the question is the same. Is there mercy for me?

The answer is always 'yes'.

Endpiece

A LETTER FROM TOMMY

Every one of us in life has a story. My story may be different in part, but all of us carry the same burden.

If you were to ask me whether I'd like to change my story, I would say 'definitely not'. If I had the choice, I would certainly change aspects of it, but not all I went through or experienced. It's a bit of a cliché, but it truly has made me the person I am today. Because of my story, I have seen countless people's lives changed. I have seen folks on the brink of suicide change their minds and find freedom from the pain of life, now suicidal and depression free. I have met many people on the last leg of their journey and have had the privilege of introducing them to the Author of Life.

One such story is a man called John, a lovely old-school man who had carried around the shame and hurt from being abused in reform schools as a child. When I met him, he was eighty three years of age. It was as if he carried on his face such a guilt and shame. I was putting in a bathroom for him to ease the pain of old age, arranged by a board in Ireland that pays for men and woman who have suffered clerical abuse in homes and schools. I would say there's not a family in Ireland that has not been affected by this. Generations of lives have been ruined.

I would go into John's house in the morning and sit with him and his wife. I'd tell them there is hope, there is a way out of the hurt and shame. I have found it; I would tell them. I have no effects of abuse in my life because I now have a new life. God has said that He can make you a new man, a new creation, and I've experienced this in my life.

One of the hardest things to talk about with someone who has been abused by priests is the subject of a good God, especially to the old-school men, because they have been brought up in such a way as to not talk about feelings. They don't let down their guard – it's a sign of weakness.

But John would listen intently to all I was saying. I would say to him, 'John, go and have a conversation with Jesus on your own. Talk to Him about your pain and ask Him to bring healing into your life.'

As I was working in the house every day, each time I went in, I would see a change in John's face. He even started talking to his son, who he had not talked to in years. God had done His work. Jesus had made him a new creation. The old man John was gone, Jesus had made him new. Five days after finishing the work, John had a massive heart attack and went home to Jesus a free man. There was mercy for John.

Mick was a pigeon man. I had met Mick three years previously. I would sit with him and talk about pigeons and Jesus. To be honest, he would be more interested in the pigeons! Three years later, I got an emergency phone call from the council to install a bathroom for a man who had received news that he had cancer and was terminally ill. I drove out to the address. It was Mick. Now in his eighties, his house was always busy because he only had a few weeks to live. I remember one day his family went out and left just the two of us in the house. In the past, I might have talked to Mick about Jesus changing your life and giving you peace. But now the conversation was all about eternity. The word of God tells us that eternity is in the heart of every man. When I was shot and knew I was dying, I knew I was facing eternity. It was the loneliest moment in in my life.

Well, here we were sitting in Mick's kitchen.

'I know I'm dying,' said Mick.

I smiled. 'Mick, there is no death in Jesus, only life.'

'What do you mean?'

'Mick, the sting of death has been taken away for those who are in Christ Jesus. You may die in this life, but you will live for eternity in Jesus.'

What an honour, what a privilege to lead one of those who has been made in the image of God but has been corrupted by the sicknesses of this world, back to their creator. There and then in Mick's kitchen, he invited Jesus into his life, forever to live with Him in eternity.

Mick went home to be with Jesus two weeks later. There was mercy for Mick.

I believe there are three questions that baffle mankind. Scientists have spent billions on it. Where have I come from? Why am I here? Where am I going when I die? I believe I found the answer. The evidence is clear; it's so simple, yet so profound. If I look at where I am speaking from in my own life, I never knew who I was. I wasn't that intelligent, so couldn't look to science for the answer.

Let me share what I've found. God says he knitted me together in my mother's womb. I'm fearfully and wonderfully made. So, if I believe this, it has to be self-evident that if I trust what God is saying to me, there has to be a purpose. I'm not a mistake, you're not a mistake. If you don't believe this, then why is there so much suicide in the world? Why the lack of hope, of purpose and destiny? I have met the nicest, richest, people in this world who externally look to have it all, but inside, they were broken, battered, and bruised and often ended up taking their own lives.

I believe what God says. He created me for a purpose, and I am walking this out in my life. I no longer feel like taking my life, I have a life and a life in abundance!

Why am I here? I've painted a bleak picture of my upbringing. The beatings, the rejection and all that goes with it. My mother and father were products of their generation and their own upbringing. They were not nasty, ruthless people. Just broken. I have no doubt that my parents loved me dearly, and throughout my life they proved that many times. When I was shot and in a coma, they literally sat at my bedside holding my hand, waiting for me to wake. I put them through hell with the trouble I brought to their door.

Blaming my parents for the miserable existence that I had myself was not true. That was something I created. But God is a God of restoration. When I was saved, God healed and restored my relationship with my mother. My mother ended up getting saved and a couple of weeks before she passed, she rang me – it was probably one of the hardest conversations I've ever had in my life. She said to me, 'I'm going to die, and I want to be buried in a Christian church. Would you oversee the burial?'

At first, I declined, but eventually I said, 'Yes, Ma, it would be a privilege.'

God puts the lonely in families. He is not the author of evil. Bad things happen to people and a lot is down to our choices and our society. God saw exactly what it was going to take to lead me to salvation. I may have been a victim of abuse but all of that has made me a fighter. The Bible tells us that the kingdom of God suffers violence and violent men take it by storm. Because of my past, I have learned to fight for this glorious salvation. Jesus is life and life in abundance. There may be times when I feel like I'm being dragged along the gravel, clutching the hem of His garment, but I'm not going to let go. Breakthrough always comes.

Where am I going? The Spirit alone gives eternal life. Human effort accomplishes nothing. And the very words God has spoken to you are spirit and life.

God's Spirit gives us eternal life. Our lives are not confined to earth. There is life eternal! I've experienced heaven and I've experienced hell. The deception is that people say this is hell. You may feel your life is hell, but that is not the case. Hell is much worse than anything we are going through now. We live in a culture at the moment where no one wants to offend – let's talk about the good in people, see the best in folks, treat them with dignity and respect. I truly believe in that, but not at the expense of your soul! You will know the truth and the truth is what sets you free. 'Jesus came to save sinners of which I was the worst.' That's a statement that came from one of the holiest men that ever lived – Paul the Apostle. When talking about eternity, he makes a statement that blows my mind:

'For to me, to live is Christ, and to die is gain. But if I go on living in the body, this will mean fruitful labour for me. So what shall I choose? I do not know. I am torn between the two. I desire to depart and be with Christ, which is far better.'

What a statement! This life in this world is only a training ground for eternity. In this world we get to choose where we spend eternity. Jesus says, 'Whoever hears My word and believes Him who sent Me has eternal life. He does not come into judgment but has passed from death to life!'

The purpose of Jesus coming was to save us from a lost eternity. He willingly gave up His life for me and for you on that cross. Think about this love – His love for you and me, that He would do such a thing. Am I telling you this because I've heard about it or read about it? No. I've experienced it first hand when I gave my miserable life to Jesus. He gave me His life. I knew I'd become new, changed, even transformed. The hurt, the pain, the sin and the shame was left at the cross. One of the stumbling blocks in me giving my life to Jesus was because of a priest who abused me. He would say I was a filthy sinner, that it was my fault he was abusing me. So, when it was said to me so many times that Jesus came to save sinners, I would automatically feel dirty and ashamed. And so is the case for many in my country, because of the effects of abuse by the Catholic Church. Many have developed a hatred for the things of God. Can I tell you, friend, today this is not the God I have experienced, the God that I have come to know. The Bible says:

'For God did not send His Son into the world to condemn the world, but to save the world through Him.'

This is reality. Jesus loves you. He understands. He sees and He is waiting with open arms for your return. Come to Jesus today and allow Him to heal and redeem your life from whatever pit you find yourself in.

Maybe it's time right now to pray, to ask Jesus to change you? Here's a simple prayer you can pray (and when you have, please write and tell me!):

Lord Jesus

I know you are alive and are still changing lives today. Please change mine.

Forgive me Lord for my life lived without you.

I invite you in right now as my Lord and Saviour. Please come and change me.

Amen.

OTHER BOOKS BY RALPH

Ralph is a Christian author specialising in biographies and ghost-written autobiographies. His books include:

Working for God

God-Life

Cheating Death, Living Life – Linda's Story (with Linda Huskisson)

Gerald Coates – Pioneer

The Power Partnership (with Jonathan Conrathe)

Faith Man – Wild Adventures with a Faithful God (with David Lamb)

Greater Things – The Story of New Wine (with Paul Harcourt)

Embrace the Journey – Becky Murray's Story (with Becky Murray)

Returning the Lost Smiles – One Man's Fight Against Leprosy (with Amar Timalsina)

Compelling – The Fight for a Faith School (with Dr Cheron Byfield)

Above Ground Level – The Stuart Bell Story

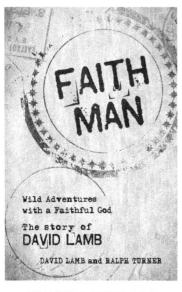

ISBN 978-1-912863-08-2

ISBN 978-1-912863-57-0

Scan the QR code to purchase and
add code **AUTH25** at the checkout
to receive **25% discount.**